Staying Above The Line
Maintaining a Winning Team

Brett Odgers

First Published in 2017
By Odd-Guy Pty Ltd

Sydney, Australia

Copyright © 2017 Brett Odgers

Brett Odgers asserts the moral right to be identified as the author of this work

All rights reserved. No part of this publication may be reproduced, stored in a retrieval system or transmitted in any form or by any means electronic, mechanical, photocopying, recording or otherwise, without prior permission of the Author. All characters in this work are based on the authors experience working with many different teams, any resemblance to a real person, business or organisation, living or dead is purely coincidental.

More information is available at
www.businessgrowthadvisors.com.au

Odgers Brett
Staying above the line: Maintaining a winning team. How the best teams in the world stay on top of their
ISBN: 978-0-9943007-3-7

Cover Design by Brett Odgers

The Commitment Poem

"Until one is committed, there is hesitancy, the chance to draw back, always ineffectiveness.

Concerning all acts of initiative and creation, there is one elementary truth, the ignorance of which kills countless ideas and splendid plans: that the moment one definitely commits oneself, then providence moves too.

All sorts of things occur to help one that would never otherwise have occurred. A whole stream of events issues from the decision, raising in one's favor all manner of unforeseen incidents, meetings and material assistance which no man could have dreamed would have come his way.

Whatever you can do or dream you can begin it.
Boldness has genius, power and magic in it. Begin it now."

Goethe, Johann Wolfgang

BRETT ODGERS

CONTENTS

	Acknowledgments	i
1	What makes a champion team come together	Pg 10
2	Innovation, creativity and the 9 structures of a champion tea	Pg 38
3	Maintaining a winning team – There is nothing soft about an All Blacks rugby player	Pg 64
4	Fear of failure – Fixed and growth mindsets	Pg 81
5	Motivating teams – A new paradigm for engagement	Pg 93
6	Happiness and meaning	Pg 129
7	Adapt and change	Pg 139
8	If you don't understand people you don't understand business	Pg 146
9	Learning to listen	Pg 176
10	When things don't go as planned	Pg 187
11	Cognitive bias, automatic behaviours and handling volatile uncertain events	Pg 195
12	Legacy – Tap dance to work	Pg 214
	About the Author	Pg 215

FORWARD

"If I have seen further, it is because I stand on the shoulders of giants." Sir Isaac Newton

I want to acknowledge the people who have contributed so much to my understanding of new, more resourceful way to live. The coaches and mentors that patiently answered my questions, my clients who come on a challenging journey with me every week, and especially to my family.

Every one of you are giants, and I'm very grateful to be a part of your lives, and even more grateful that you love me for who I am. That's quite a gift.

This book was born out of a deep desire to serve, and share some discoveries that could have a profound impact on our workplace culture and the happiness and satisfaction of our team mates.

My desire is for Australia to build workplaces that consist of champion teams. Where everyone turns up each day energised, supported and ready to do meaningful work that not only pays the bills, but nourishes the soul.

The notion of mate hood runs very deep in our Aussie culture. That's why our diggers had such a fierce reputation in the 1st & 2nd world wars. And that's why a nation with a tiny percentage of the world's population seem to dominate in so many areas of endeavour, especially when there is teamwork involved. Because winning by yourself isn't as satisfying as winning with your mates. Working by yourself is not as satisfying as working in a team that is really pumping.

And we feel it deeply when that team isn't working so well either. When our national sporting teams are all at odds it's heartbreaking to watch. When they come back from being down we celebrate so loudly. Not for the trophy alone, but when we see true mateship, players who never let their teammates down. When we see guys and girls who will sacrifice so much, and then demonstrate leadership by lifting the spirits of their team up to rebound. When we see the larrikin stick out their chin and say to the opposition, go on then... Have a go? We watch that and say, that's what it means to be Australian.

The best thing about that is how it affects the individuals. They become the very best version of themselves, when they are working together in a champion team.

Wouldn't it be wonderful if you came to work in an organisation that had this kind of spirit, these kind of values? Where you left your ego somewhere else and go to work looking for ways to help everyone on your team win.

That would be an Australian workforce that could take on any challenge, against any competitor and find way to thrive. And if we took that spirit and handed it down to the next generation. Well that's a society that I want to grow old in.

Chapter 1

WHAT MAKES A CHAMPION TEAM COME TOGETHER

One Sunday afternoon I was relaxing at my home, when I heard something that made my blood run cold.

My head snapped at the sickening sound of metal & glass on telegraph pole. And the scream that immediately followed it told me something awful had just happened right outside my home.

A wave of adrenaline rushed though me and I knew that I had to help.

I was first on the scene and my medical and paramedic training had taught me what to do, stabilise the situation, send for help and keep the victims alive until that help arrives. The clarity of purpose propelled me to direct total strangers into action. A plan had immediately formed in my head and while the gathering onlookers where freaking out I had enrolled them to deal with traffic, get medical help and create a safe zone around the wreck…. then we had to stabilize the guy in the car who was beginning to gain consciousness.

I have been fortunate enough to be blessed with the experience of extreme calm and clarity when the shit hits the fan, and right now it was everywhere.

What I was looking at was sickening. The young man who was driving was barely conscious, blood everywhere especially on his forehead, no air-bags, his left foot had snapped at the bone and was barely still attached. I had no idea of the state of his spine or whether he had any head injuries. But he was breathing and twitching and beginning to move his arms around, so that was a good start.

He had fallen asleep at the wheel and hit a parked car at full speed. His conscious brain had checked out and I was dealing with his primitive brain and it's reactions. Which is to fight, thrash and get as far away from this situation as possible.

Immediately a priority list of the actions came to mind.

1. **Danger to others**, any fuel leaking or fire. No, hey guys, can you send someone over the crest of that hill to warn oncoming traffic, Can someone check the parked car, is anyone in there? No great.
2. **Airways** - He's breathing, that will have to do.
3. **Spine** - He's moving and his seat is jammed to the steering wheel. How about we keep him pinned down in his seat until help arrives. Get his back flat and straight as possible and keep him there.
4. **Stem the Blood flow**. There were a few shirts in the back seat and the jumper I was wearing. Good enough. I need someone to get in the back seat and hold his head still and keep pressure on the head wound. Enlist an onlooker to deal with that. What should you do? Hold this tight on his head and talk to him, get him oriented to what's happening. Just keep talking and keep him awake if you can. But as soon as the initial rush of adrenaline subsides that's not going to be a problem.
5. **Get help** - The hospital is only about 1 km away,

send someone to the Accident & Emergency unit and get the guys with the right gear. Someone has already called, Great.

If we get it right we should have the guy stabilised, the scene safe and the right people with the right gear here in 15 minutes. But that will be a long, long 15 minutes for everyone in this makeshift team.

And if we get it wrong there will be some serious consequences.

Right then and there we had a team. From out of nowhere we came together. We had a mission and everyone knew what they were contributing to the team

The volunteer stemming the blood probably had the worst of it, he had a front row seat to the trauma of a catastrophic car crash. And a few minutes ago he was having dinner with his family in the house nearby. Now he was well and truly in the thick of it. And I could see the shock starting to come over his face. So I started to talk to him. Got his name, where he lived, I showed him how to hold the makeshift bandage and reinforced what he was doing well. This encouraged him to keep doing it. I also started to feed him information about what was happening and as soon as he started taking all this in, he calmed down.

It was a long, long 15 minutes until the Ambulance arrived. And our job was not over yet.

Our team had just got bigger and we needed to transition power over to the paramedics. Those are the guy with the cool toys and the drugs who really know what they are doing. The guys who put themselves in unimaginable situations to help people they don't know every day.

But I saw the same thing happen that I've seen with all

teams that become champions.

No drama... Just everyone focussed, doing their bit and doing it to the best of their ability.

We had a clear mission, a common goal. Keep this guy alive, keep everyone around the scene safe until we could hand it over to the experts. And we had a plan to achieve that.

I have no doubt had it been 15 hours instead of 15 minutes that team would have done whatever it took to get the result. We would have supported each other in any way we needed to, and we would have never, never, never given up.

What the heck is that? A few minutes ago none of us knew each other, and yet right here and right now we were working as a very high performing team.. No one person more important than the other, each depending on the others to get this job done.

It was intense, draining, and a little bit harrowing, but we did it without any of the drama that usually accompanies our modern life.

Wouldn't it be cool if we could operate like that more of the time in the teams we work in everyday? In your work teams, community teams, your local sports teams, and even inyour family.

Wouldn't it be cool if you knew that the people who worked with you had your back. Were 100% focussed on the same thing and were never, never, never going to let you down.

What wouldn't you do for that team? I'd give everything I was capable of to that team.

And how do you feel about yourself in that situation? It would likely be the very best version of yourself. You would be contributing to something bigger than just yourself, something amazing.

I used the clarity that comes to me in those situations to lead a team, not because I wanted glory or power or to gain anything. Just to serve when someone needed help. As one of the greatest leaders in the world, Faances Hesselbein of the American Girl Guides says. To serve is to live. Work is love in action.

Social scientist, Robert Chaldini, says in his book "Influence" that reciprocity is one of the most powerful motivators of human behaviour. The knowledge that givers gain. And in a team we get to experience the process of reciprocity. when we give without attempting to manipulate the reciprocal gift, then we get to experience 2 things, 1. meaning, and 2. purpose. The balance of those two elements is what contributes to a happy life.

the last time I saw the guy in the car he was being loaded into the ambulance. He was being taken care of, he was in a bad way for sure, but he would get better. I don't know how he is now, I never followed up, But the feeling of having contributed something important to someone when they needed it most has never left me. I think that's the reciprocal gift I got. It's been about 25 years since that happened and I still remember it very clearly.

Occasionally I still find myself in the middle of an emergency situation and the old training that served me so well at the beginning of my working life comes straight back.

Most recently I was surfing at a local beach and noticed a man fall from the cliff. I was the first on the scene and took control to stabilize the situation and get help.

This time help was further away and his girlfriend who was

2nd on the scene thought he was dead, and lost it. The same set of instincts kick in. Because it takes a team to get a large islander boy safely off the rocks and onto the rescue helicopter without causing him more permeant damage.

The day ended with a rescue helicopter lifting this guy from the rocks, still alive and kicking, but seriously injured.

When I think back about those situations there are some common elements

- We had a crisis
- We had a clear focus and mission
- Everyone knew what their job was
- We had strong leadership
- We supported each other
- And didn't give up until the job was done.
- No blame, no excuses, and no drama. We just took responsibility for the job and didn't stop until the mission was complete.

High performing teams

What I'm describing here is what happens when a team is operating at a high level and creating synergy. The team is solution focussed, and working together to overcome whatever obstacles are put in the way.

This synergy can be created when everyone on the team are Playing Above the Line. That means there is no blame, excuses, finger pointing or drama. Instead each person takes complete responsibility for their own contribution to the mission, and does whatever they need to make sure the entire team get over the line, leaving no one behind.

It's easy to understand this working well for a crisis or in a peak moment, but is it sustainable in longer term teams?

I've explored this many times during my working life, on the porting field and across many different organisations.

Recently I formulated an experiment with a young teenage soccer team to see if I could create a champion team over an entire season of football.. And the story of exactly what happened ended up becoming a book called Playing Above the Line.

Creating a winning team

Very few people tell me they have worked in a champion team, and even fewer have experienced operating in that team feels like.

It's rare for someone to work with a group of people who ...

- Are totally connected and focused on one purpose.
- Share a mission that inspires everyone, and
- Where the work you do is valued by your team mates & leaders, and
- You accomplish far more than you thought was possible.

While working in a team like this you'll almost certainly experience setbacks. However these team mates pick each other up and never, never, never gave up.

When one of you are weak, your team mates lifted you up.

When someone needed your help, you gave it willingly, and in doing so you became invincible, energized, clear and commanding.

In some teams you've worked in there was nothing but problems, blame and excuses. And always an expectation of... what will go wrong today?

However in a winning team there are only solutions...
Possibilities, feedback on how we can do it better next time.

Here is a truly fascinating thing.
Somehow being part of a winning team helps you became the very best version of yourself.

I've seen this happen on the sporting field, in businesses, community groups, families, bands and in military units.

I've seen it in emergency departments and at roadside accidents In my previous life as a paramedic.

I've experienced it in my band, where I play guitar, and I'm in the middle of it right now in my own soccer team, who are leading the local competition.

What's happening is the most elusive of qualities... and it's called Synergy... and when it happens it's pure magic

Synergy is when the output or a structure is greater than the simple sum of its parts.

And when you experience that in a team... *well... it's pretty cool.*

What it looks like in a sporting teams is a fluid interplay between players, a connectedness and assurance that every player on that field is valued. And it's bloody hard to defend against.

What it looks like in organizational teams is... energised focused team members who seem to love life, have heaps of fun and find way to contribute positively to their Work and their community.

What it looks like on the bottom line of a financial statement is massive increases in sales, profits, customer & staff Retention and engagement, and a team that sees possibilities and opportunities. Rather than obstacles and problems.

Teams are all around us

I'll bet everyone reading this book experiences or works as a part of a team almost every day?

The most obvious teams are in sports and you probably think about that in terms of kids and professional sports. But there are many other teams you participate in everyday without really acknowledging it.

What about your family? Which is possibly the most influential team in your life. Or the musical group or band you play in. How about the charity you volunteer at, or your church. And what about your work. How does the health of that team impact your enjoyment of life.

My experience is that nearly every human being on the planet has an experience of working in a team every single day.

A few of you may have worked or played in a championship team. A team that did something extraordinary. Do you remember what that was like? How did you feel at the time? What are your memories of that now?

When I run workshops I always ask this question. And the most common response is that it was simply brilliant. It immediately brings up deep emotions and a very vivid recollection of the meaning of being a part of that team.

These kinds of experiences are highlights of people's lives, they seem to bring out the best in them and the memories of their team mates and the adventure are deeply imprinted in their soul. Simply watching someone recall these experiences and then telling you the story shows you the deeply positive impact working in a high performing team has on people.

My previous book, Playing Above the line, is the story about how I built a champion team out of a group of teenage soccer players using the same principles that I use in my Business Advisory Practice.

This book is about what high performance teams do to maintain the results.

For you to be reading this book and to have got to where you are in your career I'm sure that you would have experienced what synergy is like.

Unfortunately my experience has shown me that there are a lot of organisations who have never created a team with synergy.

What people tell me they have experienced instead is a soul crushing, dogma orientated, fear inducing environment where they are afraid to make mistake for fear of being ridiculed by an stressed out overworked, over bearing, pontificating bastard.

The result of a team environment like that..... No one ever takes a chance

They won't take responsibility and they lose all motivation to turn up.... Which is kind of ok if you are part of a social team. You can always leave.

But it's not o.k. if you have to turn up to work like that every day, and It's absolutely not o.k. if you have to go home to that every night.

Not only do I like to work with business teams but I spend a fair bit of my time working with one of the most challenging, terrifying, notorious, despicable, conniving, brain sapping, energy draining groups on the planet.....

Teenagers.

In my career I've been an entrepreneur for more than 2 decades, I've been a film director and producer, I've owned an advertising agency and several photographic studios. I've worked with the rich, the famous and even royalty.

I've written books and I've taught and mentored all over Australia, I even play lead guitar in a rock band, and I love it. I thrive on a challenge.

But nothing on the face of this planet is as contrary, strong willed, obstinate, argumentative and downright blunt as a teenager. No one in business is as scary as these guys, not even your boss on a bad day.

Nothing will strike fear into the heart of a human being like a teenager on a rampage.

So how do you create synergy in a team of testosterone fueled teenagers? Is it even possible?

That's what I set out to answer in my book Playing Above the Line – Creating a winning team

This was a story about a real life experience of working with young men and women, and it profoundly changed my life…

…Because it became a parable for my own life and the lives of many people I work with in organizations both big and small.

This isn't just a story about teenage soccer players. It's a story that we can all use in our work and our lives

..... A brief recap of the story?

17 teenager soccer players that I'd been coaching for the past 3 years agreed to try an experiment with me. And the results were unbelievable.

In the first year I took over as their coach they lost every game, not most games. EVERY SINGLE GAME.

In the second year we were put into a division better suited to us and we finished in 5th place out of 8 teams.

Not horrible but not brilliant by any means.

Then in the 3rd year of working together, with NO change of division, NO change in opposition teams and NO change of team members they achieved the following....

- They completed the 3rd season unbeaten.
- They finished the season 1st on the ladder, making them Premiers.
- They were in front of the 2nd place on the ladder by 15 points (that means they could have lost 5 games and still won)
- They went on to win the grand final 5:1 and finally
- They won the Jim Collins shield which is awarded to the highest performing team out of all 50 teams in the club.

And they now have their names permanently up on the hallowed walls of the local church in Sydney.

Was it just a fluke?

It was a remarkable result from the most unlikely of strategies.

Culture eats Strategy for Breakfast

The legendary business leader Peter Drucker once stated that Culture eats strategy for breakfast. And that proved to be true for this team.

By focusing on culture, teaching the team members to be completely responsible for their own productivity, eliminating blame, excuse and drama from our culture, and focusing on creating a champion team of leaders we achieved a result beyond our wildest dreams.

And just to demonstrate that it wasn't a one off occurrence here is what happened over the next 2 seasons.

In subsequent seasons the same team have been put up a division and they went to the grand final of that division with only 1 loss in the entire year, the grand final. They lost 1:0

In that year they were one of two teams in the running for the Jim Collins shield again… The other team…..
……Is my own over 45's team that I play in.

In the next season they were put into the highest division available for their age group. And they became premiers and champions of that division also.

This qualified them to play in a champion of champions league. That means the premiers and champions of the Under 18 1st divisions from all over the state play in another competition.

The boys made it to the semifinals and were crowned the 4th best team in the state for their age. They were eventually beaten by a club that has produced several internationally famous professionals, some of who have captained Australia in world cups.

This was happening at the same time they were completing their HSC exams.

And again they won the Jim Collins Shield, becoming the highest performing team in our clubs 70 year history.

Culture changed everything for these young men.
While most teams focus on capability and technique, we continually worked on behaviours that multiplied their capabilities to generate a performance that was extraordinary.

Capability alone was not enough to get this kind of result. We had to continually work on the behaviours that drew out he brilliance of their abilities. For performance to be exceptional it requires the following formula.

Performance = Capability x Behaviour

We had no new marquee player
We didn't change who our opposition was
We didn't even concentrate on teaching them technical football skills.

We didn't train 4 time a week. In fact our training was just a game for 90 minutes. No skills or drills. and lots of fun.

Myself and one of the other dad's played with them, and they loved attempting to outdo us. Which they never did…. Wink!

At this point most people are sitting there asking themselves a few questions

- How did this experiment start?
- What did you do to them?

- and more importantly how can we use it on our guys or in our organisation?

This experiment all started one day at work...

I was working with a team in a music tuition business, some of who were not much older than the teenagers I was coaching on the soccer field.

This team were energised, focused and performing at higher levels than they ever had before.

Revenue was up, client satisfaction was high and they were achieving goals they thought impossible just a few months prior.

As we reviewed what this organization had accomplished a thought came to me.

Would this approach work on my U/16's soccer team?

Wouldn't it be cool if I could not only give these guys a great season of football but...what if they had an experience of what it's like to work in a team with synergy.

A team that totally support each other no matter what,

Where every player gave their best.

Where each individual was totally 100% responsible for their own performance.

And where they never, ever, ever gave up because that's what you do for your team mates.

Imagine you experienced all of that at age 15.

Would you carry that experience into the rest of your life,

your work, your family and your friends?

How would that transform a young man or woman?

And what impact could these young people have on the world in the years to come?

My mission had just got a little bit bigger? Yes I wanted them to have a great season and learn to be young men and women of greatness. But the impact of these kinds of lessons could go a lot further than the soccer field.

And so began a bold experiment which ended with the book PLAYING ABOVE THE LINE.

Although everyone on the team was involved in the entire process none of them knew the full extent of the experiment they were involved in.........Until they read the book.

Incidentally, they are all acting like rock stars now, wanting extra copies to hand out to their legion of fans.... I'm fairly convinced they think they will be famous now.

The most common 2 questions that that I get asked are

Where do you start?   and
How do you keep it going?

To answer the first question. You just decide to do it...... then you get into action before you chicken out. And that was the story of my 1st book.

This book explores what it takes to keep a champion team going.

But before we get too far into that I want to introduce you to 2 principals that will make maintaining a high performance team a lot easier.

You are going to need to get everyone involved.... Because If this is going to work in your team you'll need everyone to buy in otherwise it's dead in the water.

Let me ask you a question for those you that know a teenager.. or a Gen Y or a Millennial?

What's the best way to NOT get a teenager to do what you'd like them to do??

That's right TELL them what to do.

So when I'm working with any team, teenagers or not, I begin with the opposite. I ask them a lot of questions.

And I keep on asking them, because if I tell them to do something guess what I'll get. Yes I'll get the two finger salute, or just the dismissive, Whatever.

Does that sound like a sales/IT/accounts department you know? Or the Gen Y that you are struggling to deal with in your business?

So the first first principal is

1. ASK DONT TELL

This is one of the principal building blocks of creating high performing teams. It's not what we've been told in traditional teaching, and if you are a boss you are probably thinking "I don't want to ask them permission, I give the orders I don't take them" That's not what I'm talking about.

THE PERSON WHO ASKS THE QUESTION'S IS THE ONE WHO CONTROLS THE CONVERSATION. And by asking questions that reveal understanding you'll actually get a significantly higher level of engagement.

The real power is never with the person telling everyone what to do, insisting, shaming, or bullying others into their way of thinking. It's the leader with the Jedi communication skills.

The second foundation principal is

2. MANAGE BY AGREEMENT

Human behavioural change will be far more effective when the participants have made an agreement about what they are prepared to do. The act of asking, So do we have an agreement, seems to create significant differences in the ensuing activities

In your work group it could sound like this...
Janet, I was hoping you could help me with something?
Would you be willing to look at some new approaches to how we can improve the sales figures?

The almost automatic response is, yeah sure. There is very little resistance in this approach.

You asked
And you both agreed to what you were going to do next. And when someone makes an agreement with you something changes in their brain chemistry. It appears that we feel compelled to maintain a consistency in what we've said we would do, so they keep their agreement.

The next step is clarity of your goals
I've never seen a management text anywhere that didn't include the phrase COMMON GOAL

So in building your team I strongly suggest you get totally

clear on what the big picture is. Then get each area of your business and every team within it to work on what their goals are.

In my U/16's soccer team this is how it happened.
One day at the drinks break, after I had worn them out a little and they were moderately docile. I asked them a question

What would you guys like to achieve this season?
I'd like to know what kind of a season you want to have?

Do you just want to have fun and win more games than you lose or would you like to aim for the grand final.
After a bit of horsing around we settled on the idea of

Wouldn't it be cool if we made it to the grand final? But not at the expense of being too intense or serious, we still want to have fun while we play.

At this point we thought winning the grand final was out of our reach. Remember, this team had only just started wining games less then 12 months ago, a grand final was a dream.

And getting there at all costs was not the way we wanted to do it. We still wanted to have fun. But if we could finish in the top 4 in the ladder we'd thought we could scrape our way to grand final day. And that would be very, very cool. Especially for a team with the track record we had.

The team came up with this and began to get a little excited about it. In the highly optimistic way people often do when they find an idea that energizes them.

But I wanted to make sure they understood what they were asking for.

So I asked them the question that really started all of this off...

Are you willing to do what it takes and have me coach you to get to that goal?

The reply
hunrundohn - which is teenager for sure, whatever.

So we had our goal, and the lift in energy and focus was amazing.

Tactics to build a champion team

Then what?

Drills? Run them till they drop? Find a marquee player? Get a pro coach to teach them? What?

I decided to take the same approach I take with my business clients.

Start with the Inner game.
I decided to start with their mindset.

Right now you are probably thinking... What?

Not that fluffy crap! We want the hard core secrets of an elite athlete.

We want reps and sets, we want sweat and tears, that's the story we want to hear.

How are mind games going to help us?

BUT ...Every performance starts in the MIND!

So I taught them the best secret I had, the biggest gun I had in my arsenal, the mac daddy of personal performance, the one piece of technology that has outshone all others....

PLAYING ABOVE THE LINE

Yes a line. The line of personal responsibility, the line between success and failure, both personally and as a team.

This one secret has made people billions of dollars, elected officials to high office and transformed the lives of ordinary people.

It's also the line above which all winning teams and individuals live.

Above the line quite simply is Taking 100% responsibility

and below the line...

Blame, Excuses and Drama

The below the line behaviours is where the people and teams live that are falling apart, the ones that are imploding and are constantly hitting brick walls and failing.

Lets start with Below the line behaviours first

- Blame
- Justification - Excuses
- Drama

Here are some examples of what I hear in workplaces every day when people and businesses are playing below the line

Blame

The economy is ruining my business, if only the government

would change the tax law, My customers are crap. My executive team are a pain in the you-know-what. they never have my back. That's the day shifts responsibility.

What it sounds like in a soccer team is.
He wasn't the guy I was supposed to be defending - that was Harrys job. It's too hot. If only the rest of the team would put in I wouldn't be so tired.

Excuses & Justification

I didn't sign up for this. It's is not in my job description, I'm tired I had a late night, we don't have enough in the budget for that, they'll never buy it.
And the one we love to trot out…. I can't get good staff…. Gen Y are hopeless etc, etc.

And on the sports field
The opposition are so rough. We haven't learned how to do that. Training like that won't work. I know better. It works for Man United. I was out of position because i was tired.

Drama

Well you've probably all experienced drama both at work and on the field.

High emotion, anger, tears, frustration, noise…. Or the opposite.. the silent treatment, the passive aggressive. the total lack of empathy and the stubborn refusal to contribute.

A great example of this is the team that the French fielded in one of the world cup tournaments.

Despite having the best, highest paid players on their team they were bundled out of the competition in the first round. A national disgrace… and what did we hear day after day.

Management blaming the players. Players blaming the coach, excuse after excuse and massive bust ups in the dressing rooms. And even on the field
The result.....Disaster.

What does the opposite of that look like?

It's a simple but profound word.

Responsibility

From the dictionary
The state of having control
The state of being accountable for something:
The ability to act independently and make decisions

There are 2 essential elements to this one concept

1. You take Ownership of whatever situation is in front of you, it's yours to deal with.

    No judgment as to right, wrong, good or bad, it's here. Deal with it.

    There is no one else who is responsible for your actions right now. It's all up to you. So be in control of your own decisions.

    In fact in my teams we have a saying. No Failure only feedback.

The second element.

2. Be accountable. When someone asks you what happened be prepared to give an account of what you did, no judgment, no justification, no excuses. This is what happened. Collect the data and share the

feedback.

Simple isn't it?

But what kind of difference would it make if everyone in your organisation took total responsibility for their work?

No justification, no blame. Just own the situation and deal with it to the best of your ability. And if you are out of your depth or need additional skills, ask for help.

What it results in with my teams is extraordinary success. An the teenage soccer team was just one of those success's

With arguably one of the lowest average skill levels in the competition they WON EVERYTHING.

What about playing above the line in business?

In a real estate firm I this approach doubled their sales from last year, without changing any marketing

In a music business I worked with it's achieving profitability within 3 months after 6 years of struggle.

In elite tennis it looks like Andre Agessi demolishing his opponents to win Wimbledon

In Paul Roo's AFL teams it's Grand final success.

For a CEO it's looks like leading their organisation to a massive change in culture, profitability and success.

When you play above the line in your life and your business extraordinary things happen.

Unintended consequences of living with this kind of integrity sometimes look like miracles… Finance or capital appears from unexpected places, amazing talent is attracted to your organisation, contracts and opportunities materialize where there were only roadblocks previously.

But what you are experiencing is what it's like to live in alignment with your highest purpose.

Being 100% responsible for your

- Your life.
- Your decisions,
- actions, and reactions
- Your happiness, output and
- Your environment ....THIS will change the world, and your team.

It's a simple idea....But it's not easy to consistently do.

Addicted to Drama

Because most people don't want to change, and our culture seems to be addicted to drama and negativity. let's face it.. dramatic reality television rates, bad news leads and the new narcissism seems to thrive on conflict and aggression.

And when people feel threatened by change. They attack. They tear down and they criticize.

That's their reptilian brain kicking in, the ancient fight or flight response.

And it's challenging to stay above the line and not to compromise on your values.

The conflict I see in our communities, schools and work places is often a battle between those who choose to play above the line and move forward. And those who feel diminished and challenged in some way by change and responsibility, so they cling to below the line behaviours.

But when you stop hanging on and let go that's when magic happens. It makes space for creativity, inspiration and innovation.

Create a balance between meaning and fun. Tap Dancing to work.

Creating a high performing team isn't just about winning trophies or building businesses… It's about so much more than that.

If your team are Tap-Dancing to work, producing inspired stuff and creating more leaders around them, we are doing so much more than creating profitable businesses. We are creating communities who have a balance of happiness and meaning.

What my experience tells me is that each team member will look back on the challenges and hurdles they face, and say that they felt really happy during this time

That's because they are going through what psychologists call a flow experience. A moment of peak focus when they are challenged and fully engaged in something they believe has great value.

What the scientists have discovered is that the more FLOW experiences you have in your life, the HAPPIER YOU ARE.

Ultimately that's what playing above the line will do for you.

Provide flow experiences that you are totally immersive and will increase your happiness.

That's what creating and maintaining a brilliant culture did for my 17 teenagers, and continues to do in the other teams I now coach, both on the sporting field and in Australian businesses.

The 7 lessons we learnt from the first season playing above the line

These are the 7 lessons that made a massive difference in creating a winning team. And they work well when you do them in this order. And they work really, really well in businesses and organisations of any size.

1. We had a common goal and a clarity of purpose that everyone agreed on. This isn't the boss telling everyone what their goal needs to be, or a revenue target, and it's not a KPI's or rhetoric. It's what the team agree they want to achieve, the whole team. You, the boss, are just one member of the team. You either need to coach them through it (ask don't tell) or get someone you trust to manage it. Otherwise all you'll get is skepticism and distrust.

2. We created culture that supports the team & the individual members and means everyone comes together. We made agreements with each other, about our behaviour, and we held each other accountable to those agreements. So that we only had to manage the agreements not the players. It set up an environment within the team that brought out the best in each of us. When you manage the agreements you made within the team or between two people you don't have to get personal or criticize, you are merely determining whether the agreement you made still works or need to be modified. It is the responsibility of each person to only make agreement they can keep. Otherwise

everyone making the agreement is diminished.

3.   Leadership requires selflessness, courage and tenacity. A definition I have of a leader is that people flourish and grow around them. Leaders helps their team to never, never, never give up. So members feel totally supported.

4.   We took responsibility for our own contribution….. No blame, no excuses and no drama. This empowered everyone in our team, and we held each other accountable for our actions. We chose to play above the line and we reminded each other of that choice regularly. It's much less confronting & destructive to just say, hey guys, let's get above the line, than it is to single out or modify a specific behaviour.

5.   No mistakes, only feedback. No failure only feedback: So we corrected fast and we fixed things without any recrimination. This meant players could take risks and act on inspiration without fear of being torn down. We did not blame, attack or put down anyone for taking a risk that didn't work out. Sometimes a player couldn't resist so we just said. Oi.. Above the line, and the correction in response was immediate and positive.

6.   What gets attention will be repeated. We rewarded the behaviour we wanted to see more of. We did not come down on bad behaviour we just did not acknowledge behaviour we wanted to see less of. This corrected the behaviour without punishing people and built a huge amount of trust between the team and coach. We praised progress, risk, inspiration, team work, tenacity and assistance everywhere we saw it. The goal scorer usually gets lots of attention, but the player who set up the goal or started the movement got even more praise and attention. Naturally this was repeated and

amplified and meant everyone had ownership of the goal, not just the guy who was the last to touch the ball.

7. True communication is the response I get: As a team we were aware of and took responsibility for the quality of our communication. We lived above the line by altering and managing our own behaviour to get the most resourceful response from those around us.

That's the what, how and why…. I'm so passionate about helping create great teams.

Now if it's really that simple most people will be asking themselves why are there so many awful teams. Why are there so many youth sporting teams that are horrific experiences for the members. And why is the average employee feeling so disengaged in the workplace?

The answer is that it takes continual discipline to maintain a winning culture. It takes a leader to look at the long term not simply short term targets or stock fluctuations. And it takes genuine commitment to make a positive impact on the people around you that inhabit your world.

Each member has to continually make a choice to behave in this way. And you need to make that choice every day, not just at the beginning of the week, or the new year.

Bridging the gap between what works and what is really happening in the current workplace culture

The reason this book exists is that I want to bridge the massive gap between what we now know works and what is really happening in our workplaces and amongst our communities.

BRETT ODGERS

Chapter 2

INNOVATION, CREATIVITY AND THE 9 STRUCTURES OF CHAMPION TEAMS

Prior to 1962 the world of watchmaking was ruled by the Swiss.

They were without question the masters of the craft..

Their intricately crafted mechanisms were the envy of the whole world. The springs and precious metals they used kept the modern world on time.

But all that changed in 1962 at the Geneva watchmaking expo.

2 companies, Sekio and GE turned up with battery powered watches.

"It will never take on"

Electric energy will never take over from the craftsmanship of our fine watches.

Yet a mere 5 years later the Swiss had lost 75% of their market to battery powered watches.

And today it is almost unthinkable to have a watch that does not have a battery in it.

That was a paradigm shift.

The old paradigm was analog. The new map of the watchmaking world now included battery operated time pieces. And we've never reverted back to the old map again.

The shift to digital was a change in the fabric of the industry so profound that it has never returned

Someone asked the impertinent question.

Q. What isn't being done today that if it could be done would totally transform the Industry?

In the previous chapter I've described my own Paradigm shift.

And the results were extraordinary.

Since then I've analyzed and codified how that happened in a practical and accessible way so that it can be used by anyone.

The 9 structures of maintaining a champion team
Below is the outline of the system that I've developed that creates these results. It's written in the order that I most commonly install them in, however it's quite flexible in how you develop your culture. If you already have the foundations in place them you might find some elements that you have overlooked or not developed fully in the middle section.

Or you may have a great deal of it in place but are not maintaining the elements of the culture and so you find your team slipping in their performance.

It's a flexible overview of a program based on detailed experience and scientific research.

The 9 Structures of Team Culture –

1. Purpose & Clarity

Organizational Vision & Aligning personal mission

Calendar based Goals 12months, 90 days

Measuring a baseline

2. Managing Behaviour

Values & social Cohesiveness

Cooperation & Feedback

Rules of the game

3. Accountability & Commitment

Social cohesiveness & Interpersonal communication

Feedback and accountability

4. Agreements & Management

Situational leadership

Managing in 1 minute

Ask don't tell

Accountability

5. A Learning Organisation

Innovation questioning

Calendar of integration

Engagement research and monitoring

6. Solution focused

Eliminating Blame, Excuses and Drama

100% responsibility

100% commitment

7. Communication

Frequency and Rhythm of communication

Behavioural models

Interpersonal and organizational transaction skills

8. Leadership Development

Research & 360 feedback

Leadership behaviours

Executive Coaching

9. Mental Strength and Conditioning

Ongoing skills

Top 3 problems and goals

Time and task Management

Team Culture Implementation Timing

As you begin implementation of a high performance culture, Issues often arise and need to be handled out of the ideal timeline sequence. We have found that flexibility in implementation helps reach the goal of organisational culture creation.

Inception

- Business familiarization, alignment and research
- Business leaders Goals, Mission and Vision – Start with why, Purpose
- Team building education process – Steps to build a team
- Communication basics – Leadership or executive team: DISC, VAK, PAC, Transactional style
- Leadership Accountability foundations and practical step to creating a learning organization –
- Team goals and alignment to the organizations purpose – 90 day goals, 12 month plans
- Values creation and publication

Growth stage

- Creating a set of Rules of the game which govern the behaviour of the team, Including values and purpose.
- Team defines and articulates the organizational values and culture that needs to be created to achieve the goals and purpose of both individuals and the company.
- Interpersonal and organizational communication skills – Initially taught in a group and then implemented in departments or teams
- Communication foundations – Team: DISC, VAK, PAC.
- Accountability – Implementing & maintaining procedures to holding each other accountable within the team – Learning how to call each other

Maturity

- Problem focused processes using the above the line model of teamwork
- Leadership development program to enhance the upcoming leaders in the organization
- Recruitment and Search skills for ideal team members – Including assessment of the current team.
- Results analysis and Re-Alignment
- Strategic overview of the organizations goals with leaders
- Positioning the business in the marketplace – Developing and implementing Thought leadership
- Skills – Red head / Blue head: Managing drama and emotions during intense pressure
- Media training and presentation skills to accompany the thought leadership position

Simple, but not easy.

The most common element to keeping a good team in place is the knowledge that you can't ever take your eye off the ball. You must rehearse constantly.

The remainder of the book is a practical look at what works in maintaining a great team culture and adapting to the constantly changing environment of your teams. We take all the elements from the 9 structures and show you how to put them in place in your organisation.

Unfortunately these principals do not seem to be taught at universities, there seems to be no formal educational pathway to creating team culture. As a sports coach it is touched on in the foundations of coaching, and it is only through trial by fire that these systems and structures are developed.

Everything I'll speak about in this book has been successfully trailed in organisations and creates significant improvements in all areas of the business.

It is not complex, not difficult to understand. It's fairly simple. Because it involves human behaviour it is also not easy.

Progress not perfection

There is one principal that I see work every time we install it. Progress not perfection. There is no perfect organisation when it comes to culture, there are simply those that make progress toward a great culture.

So choose an area outlined in this book and make a little progress in your organisation, whether you are the CEO or not. Throw away the concept of it being perfect and take action to get something started today.

There are many ideas in this book that every person in the organisation can contribute to, no matter whether your title indicates it's your job or not. Leaders turn up when they get into action. And that action can happen from the factory floor to the boardroom.

Ask yourself, what isn't being done in my organisation, that if we did it, would change everything. And then go do it.

The following are our suggestions for where to start and some easily implemented practices.

Values

Over the past few decades we have heard business leaders bang on about values and their importance to the organisation. To the average employee, especially of a larger multinational organisation, it may seem to be a distant and disconnected notion.

Yet this is one of the most important areas to develop, and continue to develop as a business because this is the oxygen that runs through the veins of your living breathing business.

The values that are not only displayed in print but most importantly that are seen in everyday transactions are one of the most common reasons that employees are attracted to an organisation in the first place.

We've all heard the old axiom that employees don't leave a business they leave a boss. In an extraordinarily high percentage of the cases that is because there is a clash of values that cannot be reconciled.

Employees regularly cite the reason for seeking employment

was that the culture and the values were in perfect alignment with the individuals values.

Every organisation has a set of values already, even if they are not stated, written or articulated. These are being broadcast out into the market by every member of your team, and organisations are recognizing the benefits of talking control of that messages

The businesses that are thriving are those that have deliberately articulated what the values of being a part of their team mean.

It's a deliberate strategy to define and promote the values which are the foundation of culture for your business.

The benefit to your business is that you will attract people who align with those values. You will also repeal those who are opposed to them.

Creating your values

The best way to do this is to involve your entire team in creating what those values are.

The reason this is important is that they will all buy into them with much greater passion than if you simply tell them what their values will be. My experience is that if we just tell them what we've decided the values are they will not own them.

Values are one of the most significant drivers of behaviour. If someone is not performing within your team or behaving outside your expectations, it's likely because they are operating on a different set of values. If this is left unchecked then it becomes a cause of a great deal of friction within work groups.

Create a baseline

The best way to start the process is to measure where your team is at right now.

We use a process of discovery with an employee engagement survey which is designed to gain real feedback from your current team.

The we lead the team in identifying what their current values are based on those survey results. It is important to have those session facilitated by an outsider rather than the business owner or MD. Our experience is that this enables the owner or MD to be seen more as a member of the team and others tend to be more open about their ideas.

We start these sessions with a description of how values shape behaviour and introduce them to the iceberg model, which illustrates how unsaid and unseen aspects of team building which is below the water line, will drive the observable behaviour above the waterline. # see figure below

The facilitators would then introduce the team to some organisations that are already very successful and are totally values driven. For example, Zappo's in Las Vegas and the All Blacks in New Zealand.

We then seek to align the values with the vision, mission and purpose of the business that you are establishing or have already articulated

The end result of these sessions is a lot of raw material which is drawn together. The secret to making this as smooth as possible is to keep it simple and collaborative.

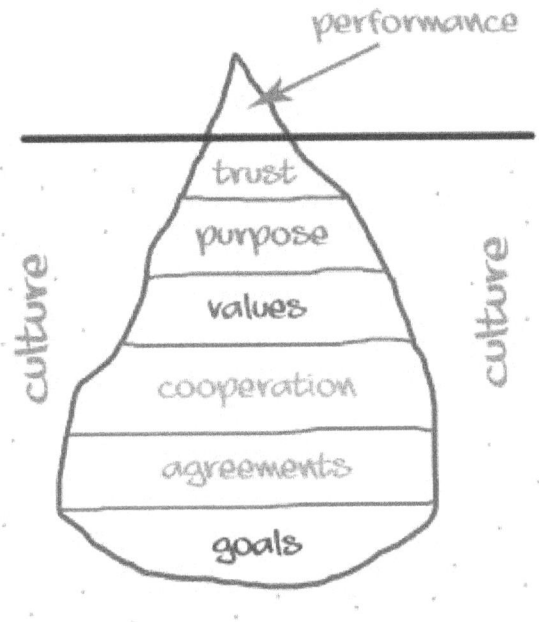

Publish

Once you have articulated your values, the next step is to publish them and let the whole organisation what you stand for. The first place I'd suggest you publish them is on the walls of the office.

Then we'd put them on your website and throughout your marketing and employment material.

Zappos, for example, have even merchandised these and request that employees get very creative about how they broadcast the values, and any of the activities they do to live out the values. They have a lot of fun with it.

New recruits also report that one of the most significant elements that attract them to Zappos is the published culture & values.

Bridging the team gap - From the Data to Results

Most business owners don't have a great deal of spare time in their week to implement this. So one of the most common questions I get is... How do we get the team to buy in but in a way that doesn't drag on for too long or get too big and onerous.

And how do we use this as a tool to attract the people we really want and to get rid of people that don't fit or live by these behaviours. If we could achieve this them it becomes very valuable.

An example of how one Aussie business started their process.

1. Clear **common goals** and purpose
2. Define **Values** and what we stand for
3. Implement **Rules of the Game** - Behaviour, decisions and accountability guidelines, revise annually
4. Develop ways to keep each other **accountable to the values**
5. **Know ourselves better** - Ask smarter questions to reveal better solutions across all business disciplines
6. **Know our team mates** - Refine what are the characteristics of an ideal team mate
7. **Choose better customers** - Do our best work for our best customers
8. **Create better solutions for our customers** - Technical solutions and customer experience
9. **Develop better strategic directions of the business** - Better revenue, profits, investments, markets and opportunities
10. Determine how we want to position this

organisation in the marketplace for the next 3 years.
11. What significant goals would indicate we are on the right track?
12. What is our current situation. How we are perceived, priced, etc. What's the feedback from our customers
13. Who are our ideal clients. What makes an A or B client and what does a C or D client look like?
14. What are our Strengths, Weaknesses, Opportunities and Threats?
15. Who are our **current competition?**
16. What **differentiates** us from our competition?

What gets practiced, gets perfected.

We all operate on assumptions that are not always helping us develop the kinds of organisations that we want. One of the assumptions that I see most often is that knowledge, once acquired, doesn't require much more to make sure it sticks. Or to put it another way. Learn a skill once and that should be enough right?

This is equivalent to taking a world class sporting team and running a training day at the beginning of the season to teach them all the skills they'll need to get through the hurdles they'll have to overcome.

It might sound like this.
O.K. guys, we've spent a full day outlining everything you'll need to win the premiership this year. Your fitness and conditioning skills, pre and post-match regimes, technical skills for the game itself and all the changes to the rules and an update on how the referee's will handle things this year. Any questions... None. Great. We'll see you on game day.

It's preposterous that we would do this in a pro sports team, and if we did this with an amateur team we wouldn't expect very good results. Yet this is exactly the approach that many organisations have to developing the glue that holds everything together. The culture.

They bring in a rah, rah speaker for a day, which gets everyone inspired and energised. Then shortly after, it's all forgotten. Employees are effectively told… You know what you need to know, we'll see you on game day.

What actually happens is a constant process of innovation, implementation, testing, measuring and adapting.

What gets practiced will get perfected. And if your team are practicing poor culture, practicing blame, excuses and drama every week, then that will get perfected.

If they are practicing responsibility, ownership, leadership, supporting their team mates, holding each other accountable and driving toward a goal that inspires them…. Then that's what gets perfected.

We have found that a combination of team days with the majority of your organisation are a brilliant way to rapidly teach them how to do all this.

We have had huge measurable success with teaching methods that accelerate learning by using games and experiential learning. This approach embeds the knowledge deep into your team in a way that traditional schooling style learning does not appear to match.

It's only rock and roll. But I like it

For example. We run a team building workshop called band to boardroom. And it's one of the most brilliant ways to teach team building and its associated skills in a short period of time.

There are very few experiences which light up the senses like performing music in a rock band. The more senses we can engage the deeper the learning.

Why do you think people come to see my band? James Morrison, the world famous trumpet player asked. Is it because I'm the best trumpet player in the world? That's probably not it because most of you have no idea if what I'm playing is great or ordinary. In fact there are probably only a handful of people in the world who can determine that.

People come to see me play because I'm having so much fun up here, and that's highly infectious. It affects everyone on stage and runs like an invisible thread throughout the crowd.
If I'm having a horrible time, chances are the audience will be too. If I'm nervous, the audience will be too. If I'm anxious, embarrassed, distracted, the audience will be too.

Music is one of the great communicators, and it's not just about the notes I'm playing.

Working in a live music band is one of the great experiences of working together as a team. It's immediate and its transparent, there is nowhere to hide.

In our Band to Boardroom workshop we take teams who have never played and instrument or sung with anyone and within one day we turn them into a rock orchestra who perform a couple of songs in a very cool professional recording studio.

They achieve what they thought was impossible. And the surge of excitement that comes with that is a very powerful teaching tool. It gives them an in-body experience of working in a high performance team, and reaching a pretty cool goal.

It's a long way to the top if you want to rock and roll.

Every week in garages and bedrooms all over the world there are bands practicing. Even the professionals practice prior to a tour. Recently I was rehearsing with my band and we saw a few famous faces from one of Australia's greatest bands walking out of the big studio. These guys were musicians of exceptional caliber, known the world over. And yet here they were rehearsing for 5 weeks prior to heading out on a world tour. And no doubt they'll be rehearsing in between dates to refine and improve their material and performance.

If it's good enough for the world greatest musicians then why shouldn't it be good enough for us.

Keeping a great team performing isn't about sitting back on past glories, or hiring superstars. It's about practicing the things which make you great over, and over, and over, and over again.

While quarterly team are important they are just the tip of the iceberg.

Below is an example of how to keep your team practicing the skills that build high performing teams and keep your organisation winning the game.

Team Days

Some suggested topics for your team days throughout the year to help you maintain a great culture & support your team.

- **Creating a code of honour** – How the military create team work that stands up in the face of incredible odd and what we adapt into our business
- **How teams communicate** – Exploring a number of behavioural models we find a simpler way to

communicate both inside and outside your organisation. Utilizing these communication skills we'll work on developing rapport quickly, deepening understand and cooperation & behavioural adaptation for your sales team.
- **Start with why** – Creating a purpose led organisation and defining your values as a team.
- **Trust and co-operation** – Developing social cohesiveness and practical systems of trust in your organisation
- **The Rock Orchestra** – We spend a full day as a team in a music studio. The mission is for everyone to learn 2 instruments, and 2 songs. Then record 2 both songs with every member of you r team involved. We also put on a performance of the 2 songs which can be filmed,. The immediacy and thrill of playing in a rock band (or rock Orchestra) is the ultimate team experience. There are no passengers in a rock band.
- **The All Blacks 15 lessons in leadership** – What is it that makes the All blacks such a formidable force in International Rugby and what can business learn from their purpose led, values based culture.
- **Extreme ownership** – Developing extreme ownership, accountability and responsibility in your business.
- **Vison led values based businesses** – together we create a set of values for our team that guide behaviour
- **Leadership games** – Developing leadership capabilities though games. Together we determine what leadership qualities are most needed in your business and then we develop those through a full day of "games or challenges" which must be accomplished as a team.

Ongoing Work

Here are our recommended steps for continuing to maintain a team culture to help your organisation achieve consistent results

Team engagement survey, Design, deploy and report

The very first step is to develop and deploy an employee engagement survey. Together we design this and send it to every team member.

This provides hard data and helps the leadership to identify in real time where to concentrate the efforts of culture development for the team

Increasing Communication effectiveness, Accountability & Results

The frequency of communication between team members is one of the most vital things to maintain. This goes beyond a simple work in progress meeting and builds mental strength and cohesion amongst the team.

Weekly or fortnightly regional team calls. The purpose of the call is to introduce, then maintain a "Winning team mentality". You could do this by either group phone or Skype and in each call the team members talk about their wins, challenges and focus for the week. We get to celebrate what's working and share institutional knowledge amongst the team. Solutions often arise from within the team and we typically see an increase in helping each other out with challenges and supportive behaviours

Accountability sessions. The focus section of the weekly calls means that each person nominates what their focus is for the week ahead. We then check in with them to following week to check on completion or progress. Group accountability is a very powerful motivator. When you tell the group you are focusing on this aspect of your job you have the whole team to be accountable to.

Speaking the truth Sessions. This communication and accountability process tends to sit outside the normal task based conversations that usually exists in most organisations. It has a huge impact on the individuals because this is where they get to "speak their truth". Just like the All Blacks Maori culture do in assessing their performance after a game. It's an ongoing assessment of asking 2 essential questions which create a learning organisation.

1. What did we do best? And...
2. What do we need to do better?

Senior Team Strategy Sessions

Go for the gap. These are regular sessions designed to continually question where we can improve the organization and keep the Sigmoid curve moving upwards.

My experience is that this works best in a monthly format but can be either shortened or extended depending on circumstances and the urgency for upcoming projects. The big benefit of this is having a facilitator who creates the opportunity to continually question and improve your current operations and also provide alternative perspectives.

We typically run these based on a cycle for building businesses that has proven to work really well. Each quarter we have a theme and we focus on where we can improve in that area of the business. e.g. Strategy, People, Marketing, Cash flow etc.

Leadership development Program - Leaders create leaders.

leadership developments sessions. Each month an organisation select some exceptional leaders from within the business and we put them together with some up and coming leaders. In this facilitated program we systematically embed leadership skills into the junior players. There are 21 leadership skills that we teach which help teams to prosper. And those are the 21 leadership principals from playing above the line book.

Leadership principals

1. **Ask don't tell.** Questions are the answers. Dictators tell, leaders ask. My favorite questions to ask the team at half time were these. What are we doing best? and what could we be doing better?

2. **Manage by agreement.** There seems to be something different that happens in the brain chemistry when you ask for an agreement than when you just tell an underling to do something. It sounds like this. *'Josh I'd like to play you in a position today that is not your usual position, Are you willing to give that a go?'* Yes coach. *'Are you sure, because I'll need you to hold your position on the right hand side of the pitch and you usually tend to drift all over the field, are you sure you are willing to do that?'* Yes coach.
When he gets onto the field and he inevitably drifts I don't have to go into long explanations about what he's doing right or wrong and I don't have to get red faced about it either. I just get his attention and remind him of our agreement. And in most cases, just getting his attention reminds him of what he's agreed to do and he's back on course.

3. **Praise the behaviours you want to see more of.** Heap

praise on your team members when they exhibit the behaviours you want to see. The sales guys so often get the praise, but without the admin and support team that sale would never have happened. Make sure everyone who contributed to the goal get a share of the glory. That way you'll see it again.. To lead your team to this you must, must, must praise supportive behaviours.

4. **Do not give attention to the behaviours you want to see less of.** There are always those in your team who absolutely must have the attention on them. If you react to this you are giving them what they want... Attention. So exclude them until they are prepared to play by the rules... then praise them for playing by the team rules.

5. **Be absolutely clear about what behaviours you expect to see and do this by asking them questions.** E.g. Is that how a team member of a champion team would talk to his team mates? Unless you give clear direction about what a great performance looks like then how will they know? Does my team know what a great performance looks like? Do they know what the definition of "great" is? If not, let them know.

6. **Create a common goal that everyone is committed to and gets excited about.** This is a foundation of all great teams I believe, without it I don't believe you have a reason to improve, change and come together as a team. It's the glue that holds the whole enterprise together.

7. **When put in charge..... Lead.** Decide and act as quickly as is practical. Don't hold back, because this is one of the critical points. If you aren't sure how to lead effectively then learn, quick. And learn from anyone you can, mentors, other club officials, books, films, anywhere that inspired you to take action and help those around you flourish.

8. **Design a set of 'Rules of the Game'** that governs the internal behaviours of the team and create a code of Honour that's right for your team. This must start with the leader, because mostly the team have no idea why this is

important or how it will benefit them. But once you have created the rules it's vital that everyone on the team buy into them, so tweak them if necessary, but everyone must agree to play by these rules or you are going to have trouble.

9. **Make work fun.** Make learning fun. Your team will keep up the discipline of the weekly grind if it's wrapped up in some fun activities.

10. **Swallow the frog first.** If you have a task that you need your team to do and it's not as pleasant, do it first. Save the fun stuff as a reward for the team after you've done the hard stuff.

11. **Make it competitive.** If there is nothing to win and play for then the intensity is not as great.

12. **No team comes together unless they are under some sort of pressure.** This is the principal of perturbation*. In a sports team each game day is its own form of pressure. So too is the pressure of achieving a goal that seems unattainable. If you don't have an outside force providing pressure it's important as a leader that you get some if you want your organisation to reorder into a stronger state and become more adaptable to ever-changing environments. This is why coaching is so effective as a model for change. It is an outside force providing pressure for change and improvement.

13. **Play the game with honour**, respect your opponents (no matter what), never, ever, ever question the ref or officials. Play in a way that you, your supporters, family and coach are proud of.

14. **Mistakes are a learning experience**, fix them quick, move on and accept the lesson. I was once trained by a former Brazilian National professional player. He said to me in a candid moment that he couldn't understand why us Aussies beat ourselves up for making a mistake. Just fix it as fast as you can and move on. What this means in the

middle of the game is, no tantrums or throwing your hands up in the air in frustration, or mouthing off at the ref for a perceived infringement. Just get up, chase down that ball and get back in the game. Every second you spend beating yourself up is a second you are not contributing to your teams game. You may as well be sitting on the sideline at this point.

15. **Give 100% or get off the field.** If you tell me you are ok to play then I expect you to give 100%. If you can't, then tell me. It's O.K., but I need to know. There is nothing so frustrating as unmet expectations of your team mates. As a leader that means you need to commit 100% to where you are leading your team, stand up against the uninformed opinions of others who think they know better, stick to the course your team have agreed on and give it everything you've got. Or let them know you are not up to it and go to the bench to recuperate.

16. **Reward and support risk taking.** Without someone willing to take a risk we don't move forward. In the Australian culture we like to take the piss out of people who take risks, and remind them of how they did it wrong and how they could do it better. I feel that's just blame wrapped up in a cultural norm and it's destructive. So I like to install a culture of support for risk taking, and if it doesn't work out so well, then we still support the attempt.

17. **Take the team you've got and teach them to play above the line** Teach them to take responsibility and ownership for their contribution and eliminate blame and excuses from their vocabulary and thinking.

18. **No team member will ever feel unsupported, ever.** They will know that I have their back no matter what and that my greatest desire is that they grow as a human, not just win a game. Create an environment that every team member knows that they are supported. We win as a team and we lose as a team. This is vital and contributes more to a team breaking down than most other elements. If you feel like you have been hung out to dry by either your leader or a

team mate then that trust will be very difficult to repair. Some personality types (I'll introduce you to those in a following chapter) will require you to maintain that trust, otherwise you'll never get the performance. One breach of trust and it's over.

19. **True communication is the response you get from your team.** If your team are communicating with you in a way you don't like then first have a look at the way you communicate with them, it's probably a reflection of how you communicate with them. The same principle is applied to the team mates. If they are putting down others then the communication that will reflect back to them will be likewise destructive. You are ultimately in control of the communication you receive from others by initiating it in a way that you would like to have it reflected back to you.

20. **Transition from one state to another as quick as possible.** In Soccer, the concept of transition relates to moving from a defensive phase of play to an attacking phase, or vice versa. That is where a counter attack comes from, but it takes preparation. If you are not ready to transition quickly the advantage will be quickly lost. I like to extend the concept of transition to every part of the game; mindset, physical rejuvenation, injuries, the officiating of the game, preparation - everything! The faster we can move from an unproductive state to a productive framework then the faster we can adapt to the ever changing environment. The exact same principle is evident in business. Things won't always go your way, but the faster you transition from a defeat to a more resourceful approach the more quickly you will grow. Likewise when you get a big win, the faster you can transition to a mode of protecting that win and satisfying customers' expectations then the more wins you'll have.

21. **Never, ever, ever give up!**

Innovations days - Values based, Purpose led activity

Each state or group develop a work or community project which captures the Why of your organisation. In some businesses they call this Fed Ex Day. Because you get work time to create a project, in a set period, and then you absolutely, positively deliver it overnight. Or present to the team what you've accomplished or created. This often leads to huge innovations in the business and has resulted in products such as google maps being developed for example

This is also a big part of creating rituals for the organization, it really energizes and engages the team and injects a really forward facing energy into their monthly activities.

The sweep the sheds program. (this could be a monthly award)

We regularly acknowledge people in the team that has swept the sheds. Showing humility and team spirit is getting things done.

When setting up an awards program we suggest that you'll get best results if you gamify the process using (free) apps to collect nominations. We regularly announce the award winner and very effectively give attention to the behaviours we want to see more of. We can extend this to other areas reinforcing behaviours we want to develop as an organization. The Ideal team player award, or Most valuable member award etc.

Strength and agility training - Implementing a system for desired behaviours

In this program we create a really essential part of any team. We create a rules of the game. That's a set of behaviours that we all agree to live by and keep each other accountable to.

This is best done in business units that work closely together. We start with a workshop for each group and then roll it into the ongoing communication processes that we set up to keep each other accountable.

The reason this is important is that everyone brings a different set of acceptable "rules of the game" to a team. The friction arises when everyone is not clear on what is accepted behaviour. This also lays a foundation so that team mates can call it when someone is outside the agreed behaviours. It is a massive piece of the puzzle is helping them become accountable to each other.

It also provides a structure and system for calling each other, then supporting each other to grow when things don't go as planned.

Mental Skills Sessions

Regular webinars that can be joined by anyone in the organization where I run through the mental skills to handle a constantly changing and evolving environment. The military guys do this almost constantly. We look at things like keeping a blue head, handling conflict, setting goals and time management. This is where we can work on skills like time management and productivity.

The benefit of doing webinars is that we can record them and they become library of resources for your future team members. It's a really great way to support the team now, and create procedures for the future.

Developing a common goal – Creating the big picture

This is an outline of a session any leader can run so as to gain a clear picture of what your teams common goal is.

This session isn't simply telling your team what the goals are, but enrolling them. While the business owner, MD or CEO typically starts the ball rolling, the entire team will have the opportunity to give input

Suggested format

1. Introduction by the facilitator
2. Business big picture – Presented by the business leader
3. Feedback and questions & Check-in (this is a process of checking in to see where they are at) High performance team check in with each other at the beginning of each session.
4. Alignment – Break into 2 groups to come up with 3 team goals, each team member tells us 3 suggested team goals or projects within the business they'd like to see happen.
5. Team agreement on the tangible outcomes for short term and long term progress

Business Big Picture presentations are most powerful when they include the following...

1. *Where we have come from – A brief history of the enterprise*

2. *The purpose of the business – Why you are in business, not the result but what purpose motivated the emergence of this business. It could be to solve a problem the owners saw, or to make an impact on a particular industry, or it could be the practical expression of something the owners values or saw missing in the current environment*
3. *What we do – How we do it – And Why we do what we do is a great framework to present the purpose.*
4. *Where we are going to – Present how bright the future is when this business is running at its peak and what the opportunities are for the future. It's important that people see themselves in the ecosystem of your business in the future*
5. *What are the specific outcomes that will indicate that we are on the right track? You may include what are the indicators to let us know we are straying from the pathway as well. This section needs to be practical, but big picture. We want the team to be able to align their weekly and monthly goals against these practical outcomes.*
6. *We will then facilitate the team to articulate what their individual (or department) missions could be that support the bigger picture. We'll get feedback from the entire group for this*

Note: This may initially seem to be an element in building a team that has already been done. Our experience is, this is not the case. A job description or roles and duties statement does not generate engagement in the same way this kind of session does. Business leaders spend a lot of time thinking about this and make the assumption that the rest of the team don't need to know, but experience shows that the more aligned each employee is to the bigger picture the more motivated they are to help achieve those goals.

CHAPTER 3

MAINTAINING A WINNING TEAM. THERE IS NOTHING SOFT ABOUT AN ALL BLACK NEW ZEALAND RUGBY PLAYER

One of my colleagues is a night club owner and he told me a story about successful opening nights.

The opening night of a venue has to be spectacular. It requires a lot of fanfare, effort and planning. The right people need to turn up, the style and mood of the club needs to be perfect. But the success of a venue isn't reflected in the opening night..

It's reflected in the 2nd night attendance. It's one thing to get people to turn up once but something else entirely to get them to come back. That requires creating a relationship with the customer that goes much deeper than just the excitement of the opening night.

I see this on the sporting field and in businesses as well.

Creating a winning team is challenging.

You start from scratch or even behind the eight ball. Sometimes you are even attempting to correct a culture that is not producing great results.

But either way you are CREATING a wining culture.

And creation is kind of exciting. It fires up the team and it's a challenge to rise up to. It offers immediate solutions to the problems you face, so your activity enthusiasm and motivation is high.

Then you get some early results. You get a few wins, or you overcome some staffing issues and you begin to increase the productivity in the business. And that fires you up for the growth phase of a winning team

My experience is that most teams are hungry for more at this stage. More knowledge, more tactics and more results. You train harder, your engagement is higher and little by little you are moving ahead.

In a sports team, about half way through the season you realise you are achieving significant results. In business, if you do a quarterly management meeting, you might notice there are less red lights and more green ones.

You've usually set some goals and everyone is pulling together to make that happen.

And then finally the scores are tallied and your team has won. You've reached sales targets, or expansion goals. And it's bloody marvellous.

Celebrations all around.

Now the really challenging part begins.

Because there is a natural and inevitable process of decline.

You've created a winning team, a high growth culture... But, how do you maintain that?

How do you keep it going year after year?

The author, Jim Collins, asked this question with his Worldwide bestselling book, Good to Great.

And now you are asking yourself the same question - How do you go from Good to Great?

Organisations and sports teams follow a familiar pattern - A sigmoid curve.

The growth and maturity phase are followed by the inevitable decline phase.

In fact Ilya Prigogine described the scientific version of this process in his Nobel prize winning work on Dissipative structures and complex systems.

He notes that all structures are consistently under pressure and the normal state is a gradual process of disordering.

It's this natural pressure for organisational change that makes teams constantly restructure and re-order. It's going to happen and it will go one of two ways. Your team will either continue to grow and strengthen or decline. But staying the same is not going to happen.

When we see the Sigmoid curve, Illustrated above, we can see a simple graphic representation of the way natural structures and organisations grow and decline.

Maintaining a culture of growth and expansion in any organisation can be done when you intervene at the peak of the curve or ideally just a little prior to the peak.

The process is that we take what is working well and continue to refine it, improve it and push the boundaries.

To go from good to great...
You need to challenge the natural way most teams go. The inevitable slide into disintegration. (the 2nd law of thermodynamics - Perturbation). And improve, always improve.

One of my favourite teams The All Blacks have a way of describing how they achieve their incredible results as a team. They call it going for the gap.

They say that when you are on top of your game you must change it. Challenge the current standards, refine and improve them.

The All Blacks have created a culture of unmatched success, in part because they constantly go for the gap. Always improving. Always challenging.

Below is what it looks like on the Sigmoid graph.

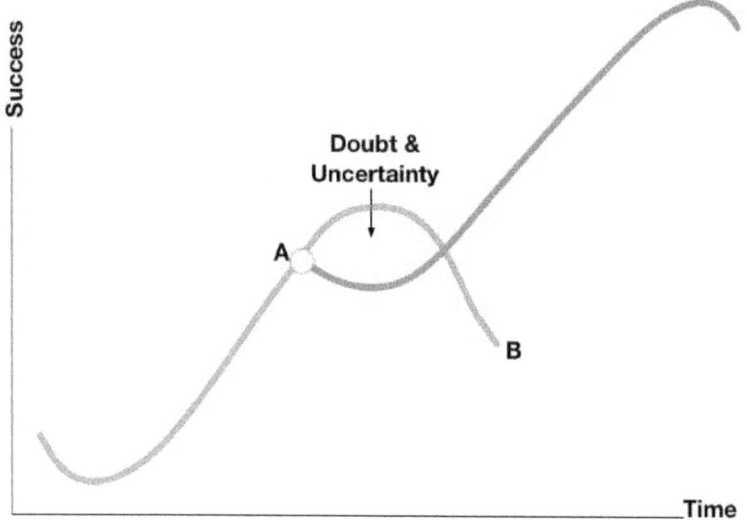

When you intervene at the right point you'll see your team move to greater and greater heights. And it's a graphic illustration of why seeking continual improvements is so important

To be a world class team, a leader in business and a trailblazer, By far the biggest challenge is what you do EVERY SINGLE DAY, to maintain a winning team. The continuity of your daily disciplines is one of the most important elements in maintaining a great team culture.

It's been some years since the experiment I ran with my young soccer team and they had their first taste of championship success. They have since risen to become one of the top 4 teams in the state.

Let me tell you it has not been an easy road.
I've passed the coaching onto another leadership team of 2, one of which is a former Socceroo. I've remained as their mentor. Both the coaches and the players regularly challenge each other, Often falling below the line, and regularly descending into blame.

They are human. They are flawed and some of the teenagers have egos the size of the state of NSW.

And here they are, sticking with it, and wining.

This year they focussed more on skills than culture and it's been the most challenging year yet? The shared purpose and sense of unitedness, trust, and cooperation they engage in 3 times a week is remarkable in a generation that many people feel has lost the spirit of hard work.

Not these guys.

They continue to never, never, never give up.
In the last game of their final season they were equal with the 2nd place team on points and needed to win their game with a goal difference of more than 4 goals to secure the win over their rivals. So the task was set. they needed to win the last game by at least 9 goals..

They are developing what the Maori culture call Mana, or character.

The All Blacks demonstrate Mana every time they perform

the Haka. It's a living example of what it means to be men of greatness.

And let me tell you what Mana looks like as it trickles down through an entire nation and to the next generation of young men.

Mr. Dawson's farewell

In 2014 a wall of young men stood shoulder to shoulder, 5, 6 maybe 10 rows deep.

The boys in front were maybe 15, 16, 17years old. High school seniors, and behind them stood the younger boys of the school. Boys as young as 12.

They stood to confront the oncoming car, holding it back from its path. Not wavering, not showing any sign of backing down.

Suddenly the silence is broken by screams, shouts and chanting….

It's a Haka

Not just any Haka . this one is for their beloved teacher Mr. Dawson.

What follows is one of the most amazing displays of character I've ever seen as they farewell someone very special in their lives. I cannot watch this scene without getting a tear in my eye, no matter how many times I watch it.

The Maori word Mana is imbued with a vast amount of meaning, but in this context it means prestige and respect. The connection of a man or woman with the earth and the enduring and indestructible force it provides its inhabitants. Mana gives a person the right to lead, and the responsibility for leadership.

And these young men, in this moment displayed Mana.

This is the legacy of the purpose driven, values based culture of the New Zealand national Rugby team.

This is the power and majesty of a group of young men standing together in, respect, commitment, and purpose.

Values based, purpose driven

Another group of men come together as one and face off against other teams in fierce battle. They are the All Blacks.

The world beating All Blacks. Two consecutive world cups to their names.

A team with the highest win rate of any professional team in the history of sport.

From one of the tiniest nations on earth, with a population barely as big as a European city population, they have come to dominate the world of professional sport.

The most successful team on the planet

It probably won't surprise you to know that one of my favourite teams on the planet is the All Blacks.

They are considered the most successful team in any sport, anywhere in the world in the modern era.
They have a win rate of 86%, which is unbelievable

But how do they do that?
It's not due to a weight of numbers. They are the smallest nation to draw talent from in the world of Rugby. England

has many, many multiples their population to draw from.

Ahhh, it's the pacific Islanders. They are big.
No. They have only begin to impact the game quite recently. Since about 2010.

And I've met a few of the former wallabies, they are absolutely massive. Peter Fitzsimmons, the writer and former Wallaby is about 6,7" and when I met him I literally had to look up like I was looking at a skyscraper.

No it's something else altogether

When the All Blacks are playing, whether they win a game or not something kind of unique will happen after the game is over.

The team will go around and debrief the game. Offering a straight talking assessment of what they did best and what they need to do better. The senior members of the team will lead this, not the coaches. Although in Maori tribal style they will each get to speak their truth, and everyone in the team will do them the honour of listening.

Once they have completed this, the most senior members of the team, the superstars will say. Right, lets get to it….
And they will all pick up brooms an sweep the sheds.

They will clean up after themselves, clearing away bandages, packing the gear and sweeping the floors.

They may be the world champions, and when the game is done not one of them will leave until they have swept the sheds.

While the press are dissecting the game and young boys are dreaming of glory and the fans are buzzing with memories of the game… the all blacks will be cleaning up after themselves

It's an example of humility, personal discipline and responsibility. This is where Mana starts.

The character of the All Blacks is something altogether different. It's not like anything we have ever seen.
It's a no bullshit approach to being the best the world has ever seen.

And they have a lot of lessons to teach us about our businesses and our lives.

There is a lot to learn about Mana, Character and the results that come from consistently improving, and building better people.

Charles Darwin, the famous evolutionary scientist declares that it is not the strongest species that survives, nor the most intelligent; but the ones most responsive to change that will survive.

That's how you outrun the natural decline we saw in the sigmoid curve.

That's how you maintain a winning team

I must offer a confession at this point.

The more I got to know the culture of the all blacks the more I could see how similar my approach to my youth soccer teams was…. Unfortunately I'm not the coach of the All Blacks… But I sure do like the way they do things. And I've seen it work wonders in teenage boys, and in organisations with teams from 3 to 3000.

The principal of the All Blacks is quite simple really.

Better people make better all blacks.

"Or the way I like to express it is.

You don't build a business

You build a team.

And they build your business:"

The All Blacks have always been formidable, but they haven't always had the success they've had in recent years.

Prior to 2004 they were not in good shape at all.
The culture that you see today didn't exist

They had hit a very low point as a team when they lost to South Africa in a tri nations tournament.

The loss sparked behaviour that left several members intoxicated to such an extent that the celebrating South Africans found several of them face down in gardens around the hotel. This was caused by a ritualised Mock court where drinking was the penalty.

Something had to change.

Why build a purpose driven, values based culture at all?

The most common complaints I hear from leaders of organisations, large and small, private and public, in business, on the sporting field and amongst communities are....

- We can't seem to get the results we want. Our growth has been stagnant and I'm fairly sure it's our people.
- They just don't seem to give it all they've got. They are lazy, distracted and unfocussed and the younger ones drive me crazy, They are entitled and don't seem willing to work to earn the respect that their older colleagues have done. And, to be honest, this is building resentment within the team, especially the senior team.
- *People are my biggest challenge.*
- If only I had some star performers on the team we'd be crushing it.
- I don't know how to make my team work harder, to get more from them.
- Why don't they get it?

One Entrepreneur put it this way....

If I could get my entire team rowing in the same boat, in the same direction at the same time.....

We could dominate any industry, against any competition, with any product..... at any time.

And it's not just leaders. Team members at every level are massively impacted by the performance and behaviour of those around them.

And it doesn't stop at the front door of your business either.

People with connections to your organisation are profoundly influenced by the quality of interactions with your people.

One single interaction with someone on your team that is negative, combative, aggressive or destructive will ripple out and effect not only the person you had this interaction with, but then next person they connect to and the person after that as well.

What you do in your organisation has an impact that reaches way, way beyond your immediate sphere of influence.

And if you are experiencing struggles in your business; low sales volumes, disrupted supply chain disengaged team or burnt out leadership….

…Guess what.

Your culture is driving that…

But Wait….You didn't set out to create a culture like that?

Here's the secret that people are waking up to…. You've got a culture in your organisation whether you like it or not.

But you get to choose what that is…

If you aren't choosing your culture, it's choosing you

and if you are wondering how you create the culture you want….

Then you are in the same place the All Blacks were about 14 years ago.

They had an off field culture that left their performance on the field lacking. It was causing deep embarrassment to their coaches, their colleagues, their ancestors and their whole country.

They had drinking rituals that commonly saw senior players passed out in the gardens of their hotels, and they had nothing but problems.

They had to do something radical... and what they landed on was this.

Better people make better All Blacks.

After much self-reflection by the coaching staff they decided to create 2 essential elements that they hoped would result in the on field performances that wanted to see.

1. A strong purpose or vision
2. A set of values that would let everyone know what behaviour was and wasn't acceptable in this team.

They decided to become a purpose driven, values based organisation.

This is a strategy that is echoed in Australia's most successful Yachting campaign to win the Americas cup in 1982.

The All Blacks purpose. To become a great rugby team and in doing so, leave a legacy for future generations.

Their values are their 15 lessons in leadership. James Kerr

has detailed these in his brilliant book "legacy"

1. Sweep the Sheds - Humility
2. Go for the Gap - When you are on top of your game, change it
3. Play with Purpose
4. Pass the Ball - Leaders create leaders
5. Create a Learning Environment
6. No Dick Heads
7. Embrace Expectations
8. Train to Win
9. Keep a Blue Head - Manage your emotions. A red head of emotions does not help you make good decisions
10. Know Thyself - Question everything so that you may know yourself
11. Sacrifice – Champions do extra
12. Invent a Language
13. Ritualize to Actualize
14. Be a Good Ancestor
15. Write your Legacy

Humility – Sweep the sheds

One of the most impressive values of the All Black's character is Humility. The belief that on one player is bigger than the team

The players are taught never to get too big to do the small things.

Humility begins at the interpersonal level by asking

questions, and offering solutions.

It leads to innovation, cohesion, greater knowledge and greater character.

It leads to Mana

In a recent test match against the Australians what was immediately apparent was that every New Zealand player on the field wore black boots. While the Aussies had a mismatch of boots and colours, some worn because of sponsors agreements, but it didn't look like a team that were totally aligned. And the Aussies lost by one of the largest margins in the history of the two countries. No one player on the All Blacks team is bigger than the others.

Wrapping up a World cup

On October 31st 2015 the All blacks defeated the Wallabies at Twickenham in England to win the world cup. The highest accomplishment in world Rugby

They beat Australia 34 to 17

They received accolades from the royal family who were in attendance. They received the adoration of millions, probably hundreds of millions of fans from all over the world.

Their photographs of their victory were splashed around the world, and each and every player knew this would be an immortal victory.

Later that night, after the celebrations in the locker rooms had subsided, a team ritual takes place. And it's quite sacred.

Guests would have been asked to leave the team to be by themselves.

They would have sat around in a circle debriefing the game. First senior players, then the juniors, then coaches. Everyone would have had an opportunity to speak their truth.

When it was finished, if you had been present, you would have seen something quite unexpected.

The most senior players would have said…

"Right lads, let's get to it"

And they would have picked up brooms, mops and buckets.

They would have cleaned up all the strapping, packed away the dirty gear…. And then…..

They would have swept the shed.

Yes.. these super elite athletes, on the night of one of their greatest victories. Were sweeping the sheds. Cleaning up after themselves and showing the world that they would never got too big to do the small things.

The all Blacks look after themselves, so no one else had to.

True excellence begins with as humble willingness to do the small things that need to be done.

Chapter 4

FEAR OF FAILURE. FIXED VERSUS GROWTH MINDSETS

The research of Carole Dweck

Fixed mindset. People believe they have a set group of talents and they are fixed. Keep secret where their weakness is. They won't try something new if they are not good at it or it doesn't prove how intelligent they are.

Growth mindset. People believe that their performance is able to be improved through education, rehearsal and continual growth. Eg Michael Jordan wasn't picked for his school basketball team

Small micro changes will eventually lead to big changes. Tiny changes = big results

Life (and success) isn't about perfection it's about *self-correction*. You just need to be better than everyone else at self-correction.

Correction without invalidation

Correction without invalidation is a concept that my Mentor Stan Jordan taught me. He directed me to a poem by Stewart Emery, which encapsulates the process of mastery so well.

There are so many critical ideas in this poem for success, that it warrants reading a number of times. It is a principal that I have used over and over with every soccer team and with my all of my business clients

Mastery by Stewart Emery

Mastery in our careers (and in our lives!) requires that we constantly produce results beyond and out of the ordinary.

Mastery is a product of consistently going beyond our limits.

For most people, it starts with technical excellence in a chosen field and a commitment to that excellence. If you're willing to commit yourself to excellence, to surround yourself with things that represent this excellence, your life will change.

It's remarkable how much mediocrity we live with, surrounding ourselves with daily reminders that average is somehow acceptable.

In fact, our world suffers from terminal normality.

Take a moment to assess all the things around you that promote your being "average."

These are the things that prevent you from going beyond the limits that you've arbitrarily set for yourself.

The first step to mastery is the removal of everything in your environment that represents mediocrity, and one way to attain that objective is to surround yourself with people who ask more of you than you would ordinarily give of yourself. Didn't your parents and some of your best teachers and coaches do exactly that?

Another step on the path to mastery is the removal of resentment toward the masters. Develop compassion for yourself so that you can be in the presence of a master and grow from the experience.

Rather than comparing yourself to (and resenting) people who have mastery, remain open and receptive. Let the experience be like the planting of a seed within you that, with nourishment, will grow into your own individual mastery.

You see, we're all ordinary. But rather than condemning himself for his "ordinariness," a master will embrace that ordinariness as a foundation for building the extraordinary.

Rather than relying on his ordinariness as an excuse for inactivity, he'll use it instead as a vehicle for correcting himself.

It's necessary to be able to correct yourself without invalidating or condemning yourself to use the results of the correction process to improve upon other aspects of your life. <u>Correction is essential to power and mastery</u>.

Evolutionary thinking

A useful approach that I particularly like is the one that Amazon boss Jeff Bezos uses. He says that the only laws he is not willing to challenge are the laws of physics, other than that everything is up for grabs.

I have never met him but I imagine he doesn't use the 500 year old black and white, right or wrong thinking when he is looking for how Amazon.com can evolve. I imagine that he is inquisitive and investigates a particular perspective, using the alternative thinking to challenge his own current processes and test if a new correction might be resourceful for the evolution of his business.

The result is that Amazon is on it's way to becoming the first trillion dollar company and is one of the most successful business enterprises of our generation.

The smartest most successful people in the world embrace correction without invalidation in their businesses and their lives. They embrace lifelong learning and accept evolutionary thinking as a part of their mastery process. So why shouldn't we take that approach as well.

If we accept that the only laws that are set in stone are the laws of physics it opens us up to a multitude of options, solutions and corrections to get us where we would love to be.

If we engage in 500 year old, black and white thinking we are destined to remain with the multitude of people who are convinced they know and are destined to repeat the same mistakes over and over.

Defending and maintaining the mindset

This is a fairly big step for a group of teenage soccer players to take on. A mindset of openness is one that needs to be vigorously defended at nearly every training. Each pronouncement rather than being put down needs to be explored.

In a typical pronouncement on the side line at half time some one would make a suggestion of moving player around. We need to put our fastest striker on. Someone would say. Rather than shut ourselves off to that thinking I'd ask, "O.K. tell me how you'd re arrange the team to maintain the structure if we went down that path?"

Typically what would happen is that the plan hadn't been thought through that far. "I don't know I just think we need some pace up the front" was the reply.

If we did go that road we could possibly play this person in that position.. And on we'd go for a few minutes exploring how we could make that work. We'd explore what that option would look like. And eventually we decided that the structure was fine just how we had it. Other times we did change things around to accommodate a particular circumstance and it was brilliant. But it always came about from looking at the whole picture not just one part of the story.

I know many sports coaches who spend entire seasons just coaching their strikers, I suppose in the belief that if they just concentrate on them and score more goals that will be all they need to win. But looking at the whole picture is essential to finding a balance in your team, I believe. And developing a winning team. It certainly was in our experiment.

Encouraging our team to use evolutionary thought was a cornerstone of my approach. As always using questions to illicit a deeper thought process was far more effective than simply lecturing to them.

Empowering your team to make positive change

Another way to look at playing above the line is to look at it from the perspective of empowering your team to make positive change.

And achieving that empowerment through an evolutionary

approach.

Just as Maslow's hierarchy of needs describes an individual's evolution from basic survival to evolved and enlightened we can use the model of playing above the line to describe a team members progress.

Consider the following example in our team.

Denial
The first level of evolution is that the guys are just running around the field like mad people playing the game, however they like.

This is the most debilitating and basic of the levels, there is no prospect of positive change, only a delusion of positivity, irrespective of what anyone else in the entire world might think. In a sports team you might hear things like "We don't win much but we have fun, our only strategy is to get the ball to the best player, and that's me" in a business it might sound like this "I go through a lot of staff, because they become stale and complacent and need to be sacked! I like it; it keeps the team fresh.

During coaching or training or some other insight, the team realizes that it's not that much fun being beaten all the time, or to just thump the ball up to the front for someone else to chase, "maybe there is something wrong!" This realization will be immediately by a whole lot of reasons, for the bad situation. This is the point that they go from a state of not even knowing how much they don't know about
playing together as a team and they graduate to the next level…

Excuses
"The reason we conceded a goal was I had gone forward to have a crack at goal myself and was too tired to get back and defend as well" In a business it sounds like this. "Alright, staff turnover is a problem, but it's the nature of the industry

or the economy or the time of year, or
the business environment in our country or the government"

The reasons for problems at this stage belong to some big environmental situation, " it's too hot to run that much, the ball doesn't roll properly because of the crappy pitch." ' Unfortunately we are still a long way from being empowered to improve, but it's a graduation from denial! Eventually the reasons for failure shift towards someone else, the people in our team. "it's not my job to cover that area of the field, why didn't the defenders have that covered?, If only we had a decent striker we'd have won that game" In business "Yes hospitality is hard, because the only people that want to work in the industry are young people that and they aren't reliable, having a total meltdown at the first emotional crisis" And now we have a graduation to the next level...

Blame

This is where so many 15 year olds live most of their lives. Shifting the focus from why they haven't completed a task to someone else. The dog ate my homework is a classic. And so many excuses are just a minor variation of that age of refrain. But from an evolutionary perspective we're getting somewhere; simply because it pretty hard to change the environment or the state of the pitch or the weather, but you *can* change people! In a business this is where the owner starts to see that he or she may be part of
the problem, part of the team that needs to change to evolve.

This can be a difficult time for teams, because the they now take their frustrations out on each other and the coach. There are few things more confronting than a teenager who has just been called on their behaviour and the coach is not prepared to accept the blame and excuses they offer. Their conversation is like a heat seeking missile of blame moving from one target to another. If it doesn't get a hit with the first target it will move to the next, and the next, and inevitably it will be aimed squarely at you, the coach.

Remind them of the agreement they made to play above the line, and maybe a thought will begin to occur in their mind. If change is going to happen maybe I need to take charge of it myself. Maybe I'm a part of the problem myself.

This is usually where they graduate
from unconscious incompetence, that is they don't even know how much they don't know....

...To conscious incompetence, that is they begin to become aware of how much they don't know, and they get a glimpse of how much better it might be if they stopped blaming others for their performance.

Responsibility
Although this is just another level of the evolution, it signifies a transition from victim to empowerment, that's why we have the dividing line and the description of playing above or below the line.

When a team cross this line they are making a choice to actively engage in behaviours that will create team cohesion and a palpable sense of victory. Below this line and what you have is a victim mentality where the responsibility for the performance and outcome is totally out of your control and in the hands of someone or something else that you cannot change. And a feeling of helplessness comes over the team.

They then start looking to outside life rafts for help, for the hail Mary options. But when they begin to play above the line they no longer need these outrageous options for help.

The "we're all in it together realization", can release a huge amount of team stress and tension. Finally the team member starts to understand that we will be much more effective as a team is we all work together. One observation is, that as each level is climbed, the climbing becomes easier and quicker, as the hurdle of denial is overcome and the team members realize they have the power to improve and they don't need to rely on outside global shifts for them to become a winning team, the power is within themselves.

In a business this is where you'll see the realization that there is hope really set in. They get a vision of a better work life, less stress and more prosperity. But the hard work now begins and team members start doing something they possibly never have done before. Graduate to the next level of...

Accountability
The team realize that the situation has been created by themselves and their thinking, no their technical skills. But if things are going to change then they will require everyone on the team to take a leadership role. Leading themselves and accepting leadership from a coach with a vision or a business owner who begins to expect more of them than they do themselves.

Expecting more of yourself and your team than they would themselves is probably the critical evolution here. Start setting higher expectations and goals, start to raise the bar of performance. Is it o.k. to just make the grand final or do we want to achieve it a certain way.

About 5 games into the season we realized that we were undefeated. So I posed the question. Do we want to attempt to get through the season without a loss. Would that excite you guys? Hell yes! was the response.

O.K. what do we need to do to make that happen? Who are our biggest threats and how do we nullify those threats?

Once we had set a higher standard for our team we needed to change how we played in order to achieve that in some games. It meant that for some games I would have to rearrange the system we played or put certain players into positions that were not their favorite so that we achieved this new lofty goal.

A classic example was our goal keeper, Mat. He was brilliant at goals and that was his specialty but he loved a run on the field. I mentioned to him that I was happy to give him a run against the lower ranks teams but if we were to achieve the goal of undefeated all season I couldn't risk the change. He was o.k. with that because he was committed to the new standard.

One of the final series games he was particularly insistent about getting out on the field. It was a critical game for us to win so we made the finals. So I set him a very high target. If we are winning 4:0 by half time you can have a run on the field in the second half. We were up 3:0 at half time so no dice, but when we scored a late goal to get us to 4:0

I started to get some serious gesticulations from Pat about having a run. I couldn't really change goalies mid half so I sent one of the very cute and persuasive younger sisters of our player over to give him the bad news, and asked her to tell him how unbelievable Brett thinks you are playing in goals today. He was happy with that.

Ownership
The best way to define ownership, is that you can be made Responsible… you can be made Accountable… but you can't be made ownership, it even sounds wrong.

Ownership is something that must be taken, and can't be given. This is the ultimate evolution of power for an individual and a team. Taking ownership means you make the internal decision that if the change is going to happen then it's going to up to you to make that change and you'll do whatever it takes to make that happen.

When I was explaining it to the team one of my resident clowns declared that there was no difference between ownership and responsibility. Fortunately his team mates replied, Yes there is you idiot! Ownership means that you are actually doing it and you choose to deal with it.

Responsibility is when someone else gives you the job to do. Another person chipped in. Yeah responsibility is about the team and ownership is about each person. Being responsible means people rely on you to get something done. Ownership is about you owning the problem and doing something about it.

This level is the ultimate form of evolution and empowerment and is the total opposite of helplessness.

And when practiced you will find a team in unconscious competence, that means they are doing things naturally and without thinking at a very high level of technical ability.

Staying above the line – Daily questions

One of the best ways I've found to stay above the line is with a series of self-mentoring questions, usually asked daily that Stan has taught me.

Going through this checklist will help you determine if you are playing above or below the line.

Stan Jordan's Self Mentoring questions.

1. What am I doing today to get what I want? am I

majoring in minors or giving the right attention to the majors.
2. Will my actions improve my situation and move me to where I want or am I settling?
3. How would the person I want to become do the things I am about to do.
4. How long can I hold my vision (being clear on your why) e.g. 20 reasons why I'm a [your job] soccer coach to this team.
5. Am I willing to accept the consequences of not changing
6. WHO IS IN CONTROL?, e.g. am I being led by someone else or am I in control of myself,
7. What don't I see?
8. Am I setting in motion the causes that will produce the effect I want?

Chapter 5

MOTIVATING TEAMS. A NEW PARADIGM FOR ENGAGEMENT

"There is a significant difference between what science knows and what business does when it comes to motivating people" exclaimed the New York times writer Daniel Pink from the TED stage.

Daniel Pink is a lawyer who is doing a brilliant job using his skills of persuasion to have us to look at an alternative perspective on motivating. One based on research.

He goes on to say.

"In 2009, economists at London School of Economics looked at 51 studies of pay-for-performance plans within companies. Here's what they said: "We find that financial incentives can result in a negative impact on overall performance."

There is a mismatch between what science knows and what business does. And what worries me, as we stand here in the rubble of the economic collapse, is that too many organizations are making their decisions, their policies about talent and people, based on assumptions that are outdated, unexamined, and rooted more in folklore than in science.

And if we really want to get out of this economic mess, if we really want high performance on those [creative an problem solving] tasks of the 21st century, the solution is not to do more of the wrong things, to entice people with a sweeter carrot, or threaten them with a sharper stick.

We need a whole new approach.

The good news is that the scientists who've been studying motivation have given us this new approach. It's built much more around intrinsic motivation. Around the desire to do things because they matter, because we like it, they're interesting, or part of something important.

And to my mind, that new operating system for our businesses revolves around three elements: autonomy, mastery and purpose.

Autonomy: the urge to direct our own lives.

Mastery: the desire to get better and better at something that matters.

Purpose: the yearning to do what we do in the service of something larger than ourselves.

These are the building blocks of an entirely new operating system for our businesses." *Excerpt from Daniel Pinks 2009 Ted Talk – The Puzzle of motivation*

Melinda's team

Melinda was a bright and very successful operator running a small team of mortgage brokers in my home town of Sydney.

We were catching up and a thought struck her. Brett I want to reward some of my best performers in the team and I'm wondering if you can help me with a commission structure that would work. I've heard so many different versions from so many different people that I just don't know what will work. Pay them too much and the business isn't profitable, pay them too little and they make be lured away by offers from competitors.

I've invested a lot of time, energy and money into training these girls and I want them highly motivated to stay here. Every time someone leaves the cost to the business is much greater than simply the recruitment fee for a new person. I'm usually the one who bridges the gap which put a strain on my time, my family and my energy level.

I could see that Melinda the issue of keeping a great team together while balancing the financial practicalities had been weighing on her mind.

The words tumbled out of her mouth, increasing with intensity and emotion as she told me more about the battle in her head to find a way to keep the family together.

Finally Melinda seemed to have exhausted herself, and she finished with a huge sigh.... I just don't know what to do?

It was clear to me that she had spent quite a few hours lying awake at night attempting to put this puzzle together.

Have you considered alternatives to motivating your team...... What other than money? She shot back... What else is there?

Are you familiar with the Daniel Pink's book Drive? I asked. She just stared at me not quite comprehending that there was an alternative to commissions... I was about to introduce Melinda to the idea that giving people more money has been shown to reduce their performance on complex tasks. I feared I might just make her head explode.

TRUST and Cooperation

As the world famous skipper of Australia 2, John Bertrand said. "Purpose and trust are the secrets to a winning team - *When you are off to war the organizations implode from within - it was important that there was compatibility amongst the team. You must get the trust thing nailed, otherwise it's like a cancer* - John Bertrand

Trust is at an all-time low.

There has never been a time like this. So we need to re look at how we do things, Time for a complete re-think

The Edelman trust report, states that trust is at an all-time low, lower even than the 2008 global financial crisis when a vast amount of the world's population had the rug pulled out from under them with the banking system.

In the past year we witnessed unprecedented signals of uncertainty, both locally and globally.

The 2015 Edelman Trust Barometer reveals an alarming contraction of trust across all institutions, reaching the lows of the Global Financial Crisis (GFC) in 2009.

In Australia we saw a decline in trust across all institutions particularly government and business.

We think there are important implications for what organizations of all types should do and say in an environment where it's harder than ever to earn trust.

In their recently released 2016 they have found that

Business has begun to earn back this trust but government is lagging way behind.

From the executive summary of the 2016 report

"There is deeply disturbing news in the Edelman TRUST BAROMETER 2016: A yawning trust gap is emerging between elite and mass populations.

The global survey asks respondents how much they trust the four institutions of government, business, nongovernmental organizations and media to do what is right.

The survey shows that trust is rising in the elite or "informed public"

group – those with at least a college education, who are very engaged in media, and have an income in the top 25 percent. However, in the "mass population" (the remaining 85 percent of our sample), trust levels have barely budged since the Great Recession

Building trust is the foundation of motivating your team

And it looks like we have a bit of work to do to generate trust in our teams.

How do you develop trust? The Sociologist Brene Brown gives a brilliant description of it in her book, Daring Greatly. She says it's like the jelly bean jars that teachers use in primary school classes. If you have a child in primary school you may have seen it.

At the front of the room is a jar with a lot of brightly coloured jelly beans in it. When the class or one of its members does something great, the teacher adds a jelly bean to it. When they don't they take a jelly bean out of the jar. At the end of the year if the class have reached the objective of filling up the jar with jelly beans they get a reward. A pizza party for example.

Brene Brown suggests that trust is like this jelly bean jar. When you do something that generates trust, such as making an agreement and then keeping your word, you are making a deposit in the jar. When you break your agreements you are taking out the jelly beans.

Any relationship that keeps adding to the jar in small amounts is in fact growing in trust and cooperation. This relationship can also survive the occasional withdrawal of jelly beans.

However if you are in a relationship with someone who is constantly withdrawing from the jar then your level of trust is eroding. And it will take much more than a grand gesture to replace that trust.

I really like this example because it emphasizes that trust is build or lost slowly. Making small agreements and keeping them is the discipline that creates trust.

In our busy workplaces it's very easy to miss appointment or forget that you agreed to so something for someone in your team. And every time you do that it's another jelly bean that is withdrawn from the jar.

Drive. What motivates your team

In the book "Drive" Daniel Pink looks at what the science now knows about motivating people and what business actually does. And it's a long, long way from the traditional thinking and commission structures that our modern organizations have set in place.

First let me get the elephant in the room out of the way. Yes, money is important, up to a point. And until you reach that point pursuing more money will be a motivating factor for you. But that point is not as high as you think.

Once we earn enough to live a reasonably comfortable life we are surprisingly unmotivated by money.

For most people in the developed world this is approximately equal to a medium wage. Around $80k p/a here in Australia in 2016

It's the amount you need to live in a good house, in a nice suburb and send your children to local schools with a good standard of education. You'll take regular domestic holidays on this wage and enjoy sports, hobbies and entertainment with your circle of friends. Whatever that is where you live, research is showing that's the point at which money will lose its ability to motivate you to a higher level of performance.

I'm not talking about sending your children to private schools and going on overseas holidays while driving a luxury car. That may seem to be the worldwide average these days, but only because this section of the community seem to be louder than the rest.

But lets say that is you and you need $150K p/a to live the comfortable life you need. Then that's your number.

People seem to be motivated by money at first glance but once you dig deeper you'll discover that is not the full picture. When I coach individual team members I often ask about their income goals. Everyone says they would like to earn more money next year than this year. Everyone.

Then I ask how much more and the answer may surprise you. Those who are earning $65K p/a would like to increase their wage by $5K. That's .07%

And those who are on $85K would like to increase their wage by about $7k p/a. That's 0.08%

Lets put this in context. I'm pushing them for their goals for next year, they aren't giving this information up easily, they really haven't thought about it much at all. So I usually ask, what would your absolute ideal income be next year, if you could have anything in this current position. What are your wildest dreams when it comes to money?

Oh, in that case I'd like to earn an extra $10K p/a

Yes that's the most common response I get. An extra $10K. For the most part our team members are not significantly motivated by money. Not one person has ever said I want to double my wage, or triple it. Or I would do whatever it takes to earn $1million next year. Once they are relatively comfortable the money is not a highly motivating force.

The other caveat with money is this. If the amount you pay your employees or team members is roughly equivalent to the industry standard for that position, then money is out of the motivation equation. If you are grossly underpaying the industry average, then money will be a high motivator. But in most developed economies this is difficult to do.

So I Asked Melinda, are your team paid the industry average? To which she enthusiastically replied that she made sure they were about 5-10% above the industry average.

Have you ever asked your team what motivates them? No, she replied. I have always just assumed that money motivates them. As a business owner I'm quite focused on money, so I just assumed it would be the same for them.

Do your team engage in mundane highly process oriented tasks? "What like factory workers" she replied. "Not at all, they need to use their experience to solve quite complex problems." O.k. then I replied, we are on the right track."

Research has shown that extrinsic motivators such as money does improve performance of workers who are working on very narrowly focused tasks that have simple rules to follow. Rewards by their nature narrow a persons focus, help them see a simple goal right in front of them and they zoom straight to it.

The problem is automation has taken over most of these kinds of tasks in business. For example. Accounting and bookkeeping, which clearly fits into the category or simple rules and highly process oriented work, is brilliantly automated by programs such as Xero. A vast amount of small to medium businesses can have a brilliant piece of software do this without any need to incentivize anyone. And there are dozens of example of this in business today.

The remaining tasks require creative thinking and advanced problem solving, because the solutions we need our teams to deal with are often on the periphery. And these kinds of people do not respond well to extrinsic motivation.

What they respond really well to is intrinsic motivation.

Boiling the research down we find that three things that motive people more than money are;

1. Purpose – Is the mission of the business they are

working for aligned with their own values.

2. Autonomy – The ability to self-direct at least some of their day and have a degree of independence in their work.

3. Mastery – Will the work provide an opportunity to learn new skills and develop as a professional and an individual

Let's look at these in the context of keeping a team performing at their highest level.

The Power of Purpose

I mentioned earlier a great quote I heard from an entrepreneur. "If I could keep my whole team rowing in the same boat, in the same direction at the same time. We could dominate any market, with any product, against any competition at any time"

That's the power of purpose

But so few teams are clear about what their purpose is. Business leaders, sports managers, coaches and community leaders seem to think that clarifying their vision and their mission is just disposable fluffy stuff. And we now know that when an employee's purpose is aligned with your organization it will provide a far greater level of motivation than simply the wage.

Dealing with the next generation

If you have younger team members in your organization then you will have had a version of the discussion I'm about to describe.

"They are just plain lazy and I blame their parents for turning out children who expect everything on a silver platter. A mental health day? Poor dears need a mental health day because life is too stressful for them. Give me a break. It seems that the slightest difficulty and they just give up."

This was the impassioned discussion, or tirade, from the managing director of a large real estate business who was fed up with the excuses she was receiving for the absenteeism and lack of engagement that she was seeing from anyone under the age of 25 years.

"They have never had anyone say no to them and they don't know how to handle it. We aren't going to give everyone a trophy for simply turning up, they need to earn their accolades"

I've heard many different versions of this conversation from so many people, that I'm now clear this will be a major issue in any working team for the next 15 years. The massively different approaches to work from different ages groups has become a leadership nightmare form many.

One approach to make a difference is to look at it thought the lens of purpose.

Are all gen Y's or millennial's lazy and not prepared to work to hone a skill? The evidence doesn't support that.

They will spend many hours patiently developing skills within an online game environment in order to excel and be the best.

They are deeply committed to causes they believe in and will invest time and money into moving that cause forward.

They are very, very creative thinkers and seem to find out of the box solutions to problems that seem insurmountable to the older generations. They simply break the rules, experiment, shortcut through the red tape and succeed...Completely pissing off their older peers who admonish them for cutting corners...."That's not the way we do it here!!!"

My experience is that these younger team members are more highly motivated by purpose than any other group in the workplace. If they don't understand why what they are doing is important they'll ask the impertinent question... Why Bother?

So how do you engage these guys. Find ways to help them live their own vales in their work.

Research has shown that people who are able to live their own values in the work they do, at an organization whose purpose they believe in, will be highly engaged in their work.

So while the board is agonizing over the exact wording of their slogans and culture statements, these team members are wondering.. Why bother?

Start with Why

One of the best ways to understand how to create a strong purpose is to look at the work of author Simon Sinek in his highly influential work "Start with Why".

Simon suggests that most organizations are very good at describing what they do, the services & products they offer. And some forward thinking companies can even articulate how they deliver these in a different way, better design, more flexible purchase and shopping options.

But the most successful organizations in the world are able to clearly articulate why they are in existence at all. And when an individuals personal motivations align with a business you have a match made in heaven.

The Elon Musk led organization Space X is a great example of this. What they do is to make rockets to transport military and research satellites into space.

How they do it is by creating their own rockets and systems and thinking outside the old paradigm of transport to space. They found too many roadblocks in the old way of doing things, as demonstrated by nation led organizations such as NASA and the Russian or Chinese space programs. So they simply designed their own.

But why they do this is interesting. They believe that space travel will move humanity forward.

Not because they'll make truckloads of money, or they'll be recognized as pioneers in this area. Those things are a result not a purpose.

Each person that joined the team have a deep belief in the big vision. They are each contributing their part to moving humanity forward.

Now how does the level of engagement issue look? Kind of insignificant doesn't it?

PUT SIMPLY, IF YOUR TEAM ARE NOT ENGAGED THEN YOUR LEADERS HAVE NOT YET ARTICULATED THEIR PURPOSE CLEARLY ENOUGH TO ENROLL EVERYONE IN YOUR ORGANIZATION.

You haven't yet found the key to inspire each person to contribute their part to the bigger picture. And this is what scientists have found motivates people more than a simply commission.

The next thing people will tell me is that they don't quite know what their mission is. They thought they were just her to be profitable and make money. Sure. But not as inspiring as moving humanity forward.

My experience is that every business I've ever met has a reason for existing that is intriguing. They don't all have to be solely altruistic. They started for a reason. We need to explore what that reason is more closely.

And that's not going to be as easy as it first sounds. Because Simon Sinek tells us that this "Golden Circle" as he calls it corresponds to the biology of the brain. The inner circle of Why a company exists, corresponds to the most ancient part of the brain.

The Limbic brain. Or the reptilian brain. And the problem with this part of the brain is that is the source of emotions and has no capacity for language. That's why it's so difficult when your partner asks you, why do you love me? All you can come up with is completely inadequate descriptions, none of which come close to imparting what you really feel.

The newer brain, called the neo-cortex, is what we use for these functions. And it's ideally designed for that. This is the part of the brain that handles data, facts and language. And that corresponds to the outer circle of Simons model, describing what organizations do. But it just doesn't move us in the same way.

Space X

Hey! come and work for space X. We build rockets for the space industry. You'll work longer hours than you ever thought possible. You'll be pushed to the edges of your physical and mental capacity, and you'll be surrounded by a team that expects everyone to perform above and beyond the expectations of any other organization in the industry. You'll be exhausted, you'll be home sick and frayed..... But you'll be working for a business that is creating rockets in a different way to any other business in history.
We pay industry equivalent salaries with good benefits and we'd like to talk to you about working with us. Want to book an interview?

When all you do is describe what you do, or even how you do it, the proposition doesn't look too appealing does it?

But if we just change one small part of this story it changes everything.

At Space X our purpose if to move humanity forward. In the history of the world reaching for the stars has created so many innovations that each new mission has advanced the human race. And we think it's time we took it to the next level……

……. We build rockets for the space industry. You'll work longer hours than you ever thought possible. You'll be pushed to the edges of your physical and mental capacity, and you'll be surrounded by a team that expects everyone to perform above and beyond the expectations of any other organization in the industry. You'll be exhausted, you'll be home sick and frayed….. But you'll be working for a business that is creating history.

We pay industry equivalent salaries with good benefits and we'd like to talk to you about joining our mission. Want to book an interview?

Completely different isn't it.
We are all ready to go and do whatever they need us to do, sweep floors, get coffee, whatever… because if moving humanity forward gives you a chance to live out your values then you will be a very, very engaged employee. No matter what the task or the conditions.

When you communicate what your purpose is and enable your team to demonstrate and live out their values you will attract those who believe what you believe, both as customers and as employees.

A wall or a Cathedral

It's the difference between building a wall and building a cathedral. Simon Sinek relays the story of two stone masons in his book.

Consider the story of two stonemasons. You walk up to the first stonemason and ask, "Do you like your job?" He looks up at you and replies, "I've been building this wall for as long as I can remember. The work is monotonous. I work in the scorching hot sun all day. The stones are heavy and lifting them day after day can be backbreaking. I'm not even sure if this project will be completed in my lifetime. But it's a job. It pays the bills." You thank him for his time and walk on.

About thirty feet away you walk up to a second stonemason. You ask him the same question, "Do you like your job?" He looks up and replies, "I love my job. I'm building a cathedral.

Sure, I've been working on this wall for as long as I can remember and yes, the work is sometimes monotonous. I work in the scorching hot sun all day. The stones are heavy and lifting them day after day can be backbreaking. I'm not even sure if this project will be completed in my lifetime.

But I'm building a cathedral."

Landing a rocket back on earth

In the middle of the afternoon of December 22nd 2015 while the rest of the world was consumed with the crazy Christmas rush of presents, family dinners and finishing up work and for the holidays, about 2500 people gathered in the gargantuan Space X facility in Hawthorn, California to watch a historic world first attempt to launch a rocket into orbit, then land the first stage of that rocket safely back on earth to be reused again.

It's the stuff of science fiction and we might gloss over the significance of this because of the computer generated imagery we accept as real in our movies and television viewing.

Just launching a rocket is incredibly difficult. That's why it has been the exclusive pursuit of nations such as China, Russia and the United Sates of America. They have an unlimited budget for things to go wrong and still keep on going.

Then along came the team at Space X whose stated mission is to colonize Mars, but found that existing suppliers of rockets & space technology were not affordable for the budget of this privately held company.

So they decided to make their own technology from scratch. Build their own rockets. How hard can it be? We've been putting people into space for decades.

Then the first rocket exploded in flames early in it's flight. After months of around the clock work by the brightest minds in the country they saw their hard work go up in a huge ball of spectacular fireworks.

They sort of expected that. Well it probably more accurate to say they learned a lot from this first failure. They used the feedback and lessons to put into the 2nd rocket. And the boss said their budget could afford 3 rockets to fail before they ran out of money.

So back to work.

The 2nd launch cleared the tower, making it's way up toward low orbit, the 1st stage separated and then a tiny oscillation became a death wobble and Boom! A miscalculation of only 1% thrust in the power of the 2nd stage forced a RUD. (Rapid Unscheduled Disassembly)

With their backs to the wall, a third unsuccessful rocket launch nearly put the fledgling company under. It was extremely difficult to simply get off this earth, never mond getting to mars and back over and over again.

However, just like an elite athlete with their eye on the big picture they finally got a successful launch. Then another, and another. And 10 years later we are watching this team of believers attempt something nearly beyond comprehension. Launch and return a rocket to earth... Intact and able to be reused.

The most brilliant minds of this generation are working on this project day and night. And make no mistake, working for Space X is no picnic. They are worked to exhaustion, regularly pulling all nighters. The boss, Elon Musk will be in there working on weekends and the leadership expect you to do the same.

If you want to work here it's not enough for you to be brilliant. You also need to be resourceful.

The recruitment policy of this business means they are looking for engineers who are at the top of their academic powers, and have started project after project to put their minds into practical use. They want to see a history of problem solving deep in your DNA.

When I think of what it's like to work here I'm reminded of my all time favorite recruitment ad. Earnest Shackleton was looking for men who could last a bitter winter on his polar expedition. He didn't want anyone on the trip that were not capable of handling the extreme conditions. And his ad read like this.

> "Men wanted for hazardous journey. Low wages, bitter cold, long hours of complete darkness. Safe return doubtful. Honour and recognition in event of success"

And they was stranded on the ice for months, with the crew making a suicidal journey in a tiny rowing boat to find help... and yet not one of them perished. Because they were the right men for the job and they believed in the purpose of what they were doing.

While you wont be stranded in pack ice if you go to work for space X, you will endure problems that would stump most people, you'll be asked to deliver projects in timeframes that are likely unreasonable, and you will be working on the edge of your endurance.

And yet in December 2015 I'm looking at a sea of faces that have crowded around the double story glass walled mission control room in the middle of the space X facility. Most look to be under 30year old. And everyone of them have contributed something amazing to the launch that is about to happen.

The entire room is on edge as the countdown nears blast off. Some of the onlookers are laughing with excitement while the control room crew are intense and focused as the systems checks are complete.

Will this explode on the launch pad?

How high might it get before we can breath easily?

Will the payload it's carrying arrive safely to it's destination? And will every system that they've designed work perfectly so that this rocket will do something that mankind has been dreaming of for all time.

Watching the footage you can see the synergy in the room. Everything working perfectly together so that the sum of their efforts is much, much more than one individual can do alone.

Five
Four
Three
Two
One

And then it lifts off. Clearing the launch structures.

A cheer goes up, but they've seen this happen many times. So it's a little restrained. It would be a few minutes before they'll know if this launch is to be successful.

The first stage separates and the payload goes onto it's destination, and now the real tension starts.

Then someone spots it. The huge fireball of the returning rocket and the whole cavernous facility erupts as the rockets boosters fire up to slow the descent back to earth. I can see girls praying, guys pumping their fists.. you can see the tension in the faces of the team....Come on, you can do it.

The blasters are screaming now with the rocket only a few hundred meters off the ground. The tripod like legs extend and this fireball lowers the rocket gently back onto earth. And suddenly there is quiet. The rocket is standing tall on the Launchpad....

The crowd goes berserk, people are jumping all over each other, high fives everywhere. People are totally overcome with emotion. People are hugging anyone they can find, others are calling their friends jumping up and down with pure joy. One technician simply raises both fists in the air while others run around the control room screaming with delight at their teammates outside.

Men & women of all ages, backgrounds and heritages are sharing this incredible moment together. Double high fives from the leaders to the teams are everywhere. Yet other control operators just smile a deeply satisfied smile. Months and even years of hard work have all culminated in this shared moment by the entire team. And it's beautiful.

This is the moment that the space X team have built their cathedral. Each and everyone of them have been toiling away on challenges that would have kept them up for many sleepless nights, and now they were able to stand back and look at their Cathedral.

The long days and nights forgotten, the frustrations, failures and setbacks have been conquered. Their purpose, their mission is complete. And there is nothing that will motivate them to continue more than the sense of being a part of this amazing endeavor.

You can watch the video of this historic event here.
https://youtu.be/ANv5UfZsvZQ

But I'm not making Rockets?

Is what Melinda said to me after telling her about the space X story. My little business isn't that grand. When we get it right there aren't 2500 people in a hanger cheering us on. and the worlds media aren't reporting our every move.

You're right, and I know you have a purpose for this business that's bigger than simply finding someone a good rate on a home loan.

A look came over her face which told me I was right.

Why did you start this business in the first place?

And before you tell me the history of how you moved from this organization to that until you finally went out on your own. Or that you want to earn a good living doing something you are good at. What I really want to know is, In a country where you can make a very good living doing ANYTHING, why this industry, and why this type of business?

Well if I'm really honest about it, this work is really about freedom.

Initially it was about creating financial freedom for me. What we do is to help people gain their freedom. Giving them control over their destiny, their financial future and where they'll bring up their family. They come in here not knowing which way to turn and we give them clarity.

I guess that's our mission. And the team I have around me are really committed to that.

So how can you motivate your team now that you know that? How many ways can you find to help your team demonstrate their values of helping people create freedom?

Your team stay with you because they believe what you believe about helping people. So step 1 is to articulate what that is, get your people involved to give their perspective and input. Then start telling everyone about it.

And what tangible goals would be a great measure that you are in track to helping people gain clarity and freedom. Because that's a very real and tangible marker of your success?

While we are at it, what about autonomy and mastery as a motivating force. Rather than commissions is it possible to reward them with greater autonomy? What could that look like?

What skills do your team want to learn? And if you helped them master those skills you'll find that their performance improves. Could you take part of the money you were going to pay in commission and put it toward some further professional development. Or even personal development.

One team I work with will support their team members learning 1 new skill every year. They will pay to help them master new things, even if that's got no direct relevance to the work they do.

A receptionist told me that last year her organization paid for her to have guitar lessons, and this year she wanted to learn how to sail. And she LOVED working for this business.

What difference does it really make?

During a conference the guy up on stage wanted to find a way to demonstrate this. He loved a little bit of audience interaction and he later tells us that amazing things just seem to happen when he breaks that fourth wall and starts getting real with the attendees.

Today he was chatting with a guy who was a singing teacher. Sing us a few bars of something, he implored. The man was African American and had the most magnificent voice, so he started singing Amazing grace. It was pitch perfect, and technically correct as he began to sing.... "how sweet the sound, that saved a wretch like me...."

But the guy on stage wanted more.
"So that was nice. Thank you. But I want to see if you have another version in you."

Could you give me the version of that song where you've just survived a an awful time in your life, where you were abandoned, and people gave up on you. Where you thought you were nothing. A version where you are putting it all on the line to show the world what you are really made of. Have you got that version in you?"

Then from another place altogether came the most heavenly sound. This man sang Amazing Grace with such passion, so much heart, that every word was soaked in emotion, every phrase expressed the pain and struggle. It simply took my breath away and brought a tear to my eye.

And then he turned it around to imbue the song with a triumphant quality that spoke with a thousand words about how this song tells the story of the human spirits ability to overcome anything.

It was no longer simply the words and the notes with the familiar tune we all know. It had purpose behind it, and the room was transformed.

When he knew why he was singing this song it totally transformed how he sang it. And had a profound effect on everyone who heard him perform it this way.

When you know why you do the work you do, it transforms how you accomplish all the little tasks that are required to complete you role.

Some practical guidance for finding your why

You already have a purpose whether you have articulated it or not. You have a culture as well, even if you haven't designed it. The question you must ask is... How resourceful is the culture we currently have. Is the purpose we are currently speaking about engaging our business at all levels.

If you are focused on figures and numbers then your team will assume this is your companies why. If it's about winning awards, your team will assume this is your why.

Every company has a deeper reason as to what motivates them to work. Your job is to find out what that is an begin to integrate that into every area of your business, because that's what the most successful organisations on the planet do.

And the way to approach that is a little bit at a time.
It would be really cool if you suddenly hit on an idea that

everyone agreed was it. But that's not how it usually works in the real world.

Start with ideas from everyone. Get the input of people who have been at your company for a long time, and also find out what exactly it was that attracted some of the newer people.

Ask questions of the founders as to why they started this business. Not how they did it or what they did, but what motivated them. That's where the purpose is.

The great world war 2 General, George Patton once said.

" An imperfect plan violently executed right now is better than a perfect plan next week"

Progress is far more important than perfection. So start with the imperfect description of your purpose. Get feedback from everyone and debate it amongst yourselves.

You could ask individuals to complete this sentence

I get up in the morning to ……

And answer this about 5 times. It will help you get down to the reason you work in this place at this time.

Start building stories

Stories are the way that people most effectively communicate ideas. So how about you create stories around your why. These become folklore and add to your history.

And then once you have a clear idea of what your why is we need to simplify it.

Long mission statement don't really inspire your team.

Something that fits on a T-shirt is a much more effective way to tell the story of your why.

The Biggest threat to your organisation is not from external forces

Change is affecting every business at every level and it doesn't look to be slowing down any time soon.

Traditionally in business and in most teams we think of change as coming from external forces. Changes in consumer buying trends, price expectations. Changes in sporting team opposition players or coach staff or the expectations of the supporters

I see a very different picture. Yes, organizations of all types are under pressure to change and adapt to different external forces.

Industries, businesses and community groups that once looked to be invincible are being swept away in what seems an instant, and its usually coming from where you'd least expect it.

The thing that holds most great enterprises back is *internal, not external.*

I work with a great cross section of businesses that are growing fast and the top frustrations they are asking me about are

- How do we remain connected and focused as we grow? When we were smaller it was great fun. But how do we all keep moving in the same direction now that we are larger.

- And if you have worked in an organization for a while I find team members saying things like. I liked it better when we were smaller.

- Or they ask, what's the future really look like? Do I have an outstanding future here?

- Or … when we are all rowing in the same direction we seem to be invincible, How do we keep that up?

Organizations are very focused on what they do or sell. But very few are communicating why they exist in the first place

Every law firm tells us they do business law, or family law

Product manufacturers tell us the benefits of their product over the competitors. App developers are telling us all the cool things their new software does.

If you ask an accountant about their business they'll tell you who they work for or what services they provide. Tax returns or they work in the construction industry.

Some will even explain how they deliver their service in a different way.. in Sales speak that's the benefits to the customer rather than the features of the product.

But a few companies are communicating very differently from everyone else. They are communicating why they do what they do. They have taken the "start with why" concept and created a meaningful purpose for the business.

While that's great theology for the business, the real impact is being seen in the results that the teams are able to achieve.

People come to work for your organisation not because of what it stands for...... But how working for you reflects on them.

The fact that you've articulated a value they hold dear has given your team members a clear way to tell the world who THEY are.

It's what the purpose says about them that matters. People come to work for Space X because that is an expression of who they are. It's a statement to the world that they are someone who sees themselves and pushing the boundaries of science and engineering.

Yes the organisations values must align with their values, because humans find it very difficult to live in an environment of vastly different values. But when you understand why you do the work you do then you can attract people who believe what you believe. And then empower them to tell the world. THIS IS WHO I AM!

The Americas Cup 1983 Sailing challenge

One of the best examples of a purpose driven enterprise is the story of a team of Sailors who challenged for the America's cup back in 1983.

An amazing man called John Bertrand was their skipper and I had the privilege of being with John Bertrand at a conference recently and spoke to him personally afterwards and was very taken by this comment.

> ... *"When you are off to battle, most organizations implode from within - it's important that there is compatibility amongst the team. You must get the trust thing nailed; otherwise it's like a cancer."*

Let me take you back to September 1983, John Bertrand was in the middle of the fight of his life.

He was the upstart from Australia who was challenging for the Americas Cup Yachting race.

He was up against an opponent who had been enjoying the longest winning streak in History. 132 years. And the skipper of that boat did not want to become known as the captain who lost the Americas Cup.

And they were ruthless and unrelenting in their efforts to make certain it stayed that way.

And where we start the story Australia are on the verge of being sent home as failures. Right now things looked really grim.

Australia were 3:1 down in a best of 7 series; and their opposite number, *American Skipper, Dennis Conner,* knew he had the power.. the might and the legal wrangling of the New York yacht club behind him.

No contender in history had ever upset the Americans like the current team sailing Australia 2.

But right now; onboard things not looking good. If they didn't win this race they were being sent home.

As they were getting prepared for the start and unthinkable mistake happened and put them 30sec behind the Americans, or the red boat, as they called them.

John absolutely raged at his mistake. He totally lost his lolly over his initial blunder... And then something quite amazing happened. One of the quietest crew members said in a totally deadpan voice... "*O.K. John, now that's out of the way, lets go and beat up on the Yanks*"

They all laughed, The grim mood lifted, and Every member of the crew slipped into another gear, relying on thousands of hours of not just technical training, but learning to work together as a team.

They won that race in record time....

And the Americans freaked out.

They put one hurdle after another in front of them. They attempted to make legal arguments to keep them out of contention, and they played really dirty on the water.

The Opponents skipper Dennis Conner was a raging bull of a man, and towered over his boat. His crew terrified to make a mistake.

He was prepared to do ANYTHING not to be the man who lost the Americas cup.

The Australian Crew on the other hand were led by a vision. To bring the Cup home to Australia after the Yanks had geld onto it for 132 years.

So strong was the Vision that Johns Grandmother has declared a few decades earlier, that until her Johnny was at the Helm that cup was not going to come home to Australia.

So they came up with an interesting strategy

I had the great privilege of hearing him speak at a conference recently and he said...

"In any 20 year period of history, what we think is impossible becomes normal in 20 years' time."

"We determined that to bring the cup home we needed to think, act and work like we were 20 years ahead of our time"

"That meant three things to be world class., better than anything experienced now or in the next 20 years for that matter.

1. The Administration
2. The technology and
3. The team"

The challenge was well under way with the now famous winged keel and other technology that was way ahead of its time. The administration was well supported by the charismatic syndicate founder, Alan Bond. But it was in the team that John had to really put some work into if their dream was going to pan out.

"I decided to employed a *sports psychologist to teach me how to manage and motivate* my team and bring out the best in them." John said

Apparently Bondy, who was the owner of the syndicate, had second thoughts about whether he'd hired the right man for the job when he'd heard about this spots psychologist. He thought that if my skipper needs a sports psychologist then maybe he's not up to the job.

But in the middle of the next 3 races, there was nothing the administration or the technology could to carve out the extra seconds they needed to bring the cup home.

It was going to some down to leadership and teamwork.

Australia won the next race, making it 2:3

The Crew of the red boat were starting to fear the Aussies, and the New York Yacht Club went apoplectic.

They protested, they held press conferences calling us cheats, they maneuvered and attempted it alter the rules, but they couldn't stop Australia 2

In the next race the AUSTRALIANS tied the series, to bring it to 3:3.

And still the Americans tried to knobble the Aussies.

The Americans were very, very attached to winning that race.

They even continued legal challenges right up to a few hours before the race.

Real leadership

John told us the story about the then Prime minister Bob Hawke who came to see him as the crew were heading off for the final race.

Mr. Hawke asked John what he was going to do. John respectfully replied. Well Mr. prime minister…. We're going to do our best....

To which Bob Hawke replied.... bullshit... Destroy the bastards.

And that's exactly what they did. Taking the cup off the Americans after 132 years.

The greatest team performance in 200 years

The Americas' cup win was voted The greatest team performance in 200 years in any Australian sporting endeavor.

Winning the race had such a profound effect on Australians that many can tell you exactly where they were when the last race was won.

I can. I was in my year 10 classrooms, on Block B, with my English class with Miss Voss. I can recall every element of that moment.

More people were naturalized and became Australian Citizens following that victory than at any other time in Australia's history.

Because this race, this endeavor, this challenge gave them a reason to feel proud, and to be part of something bigger than themselves.

 Part of a nation who were world-beaters.

Australians who could take on the biggest competitors in the world..... and win.

Australians who could overcome insurmountable odds..... and win.

A team who could face every challenge thrown at them..... and win.

This was a vision led endeavor. A sporting event with a purpose

And it changed our nations view of ourselves.

Because of their ability to take on goliath and win there are more Australians on the world stage now. On The screen, In business, and the sporting field.

We are a nation with a fraction of the world's population and resources, yet we count for unusually high numbers in the elite sporting, entertainment and business ranks.

Thanks in no small part, to the psychology of winning that The Australia 2 team taught us

A different perspective

What if.... you were part of something that was much bigger than just you

What if.... this wasn't where you came to work, but where you came to show the world what you are capable of

Would that change the way you turn up to work?

Most people go to work to receive something. A Pay cheque, Recognition, power or reward... Cars, computer, phones travel.

And there is nothing fundamentally wrong with that…….. But to move toward greatness it's going to take a shift in thinking.

Some of you are reading this book because you want to be inspired.

But what if it's not about that?

What if it's actually about **BEING the source of the inspiration**

And some people are reading this book because they are looking for opportunity.

What if….

What if working in your organisation is actually about CREATING THE OPPORTUNITY

And

What if …. it's NOT about **BEING** different, or **looking** different.

What if….. it's actually about **making a difference**

How would that perspective change your contribution to your team?

Chapter 6

HAPPINESS AND MEANING

Mihaly Csikszentmihalyi grew up in Europe during the second world war. After it was all over he began to see the world around him in a different light, clearly he had a natural inquisitiveness that would help him become one of the world's leading scientists, one of the leaders in positive psychology in the decades to come. As a young child he realized so few of the grown-ups he knew were able to withstand the tragedies that the world visited on them.

He saw how few of them could take on a normal contented and happy life after the war. He became fascinated with what contributed to a life that was meaningful and satisfied. He wondered what contributed to happiness.

He tried to understand it from many different perspectives, art, religion, politics. He ended up encountering Psychology and the thinking of Carl Jung in a chance encounter in a ski resort. He attended a free lecture that he thought was about flying saucers. But was in fact a treatise by Jung about how Europeans, so traumatized by war were beginning to project their psyche into the sky. To see flying saucers and following bizarre religions as a way to regain some sense of order after the chaos of war.

He continued to study psychology and the source of happiness.

Money was initially thought to be a huge contributor to happiness, but one scientific study which looked at peoples happiness from 1956-1998 as their wealth rose threefold found that this did not make the difference that it was first thought to make.

After a certain basic point, which corresponds to just above the average wage, and in todays dollars is probably around $70K p/a in wages. Material gain doesn't seem to contribute significantly to happiness after a certain point.

Where, then do we feel really happy was the question he chased the answer to.

He studied creative people because they appeared to be doing work that they felt was meaningful rather than expecting financial return.

One musician provided a very useful explanation that provided some enlightenment. This musician described entering a state of ecstasy.

The original Greek meaning of the word ecstasy means to experience an altered reality, to step into another dimension.

So much of what we know about ancient civilizations we know through their ecstasies. The Mayans temples, the pyramids of Egypt and the great circuses of the roman empire. We know about their theatres and arenas and these are the places people went to experience a different reality to their normal everyday. We don't tend to know about ancient civilizations from their average everyday activities.

But this musician was experiencing the same altered reality just by creating music. He was entering a different reality, a state of ecstasy. Not only that but his experience of creating something that had never been heard before, this state of ecstasy, was so intense that everything else seemed to become less important and fade away, he lost track of time and his own physical needs seemed unimportant. He described it in a kind of romantic way but in fact there is science to what was happening to him.

The human brain is only capable of processing so much data every second, and it's roughly equivalent to 2 people talking. To hear and process that information takes up every bit of processing power you have. When this musician was completely engaged in this process of creating something new he doesn't have enough attention left over to monitor how his body feels or to keep track of time, or his problems at home, or even if he is hungry or tired. His identity is not able to be monitored so his reality seems to be temporarily suspended, even his movements seem automatic and to be happening by themselves.

The musician tells of his hand writing notes as if it was happening by itself. For this he must have a high level of skill in his musicianship because if you or I entered this creative state without the necessary skill I don't think the notes would be so beautifully arranged. The immersion in the field of excellence you are engaged in must be significant, you must be highly skilled.

So many people described this experience as a spontaneous flow that he began to describe this altered state as a "flow experience"

Athletes and sports people who were part of the study often described this as being in the zone, that the conditions were such that everything clicked, everything felt good and easy. They described it like opening a door

Business people also described the experience, they defined success that helped others and at the same time contributed to feeling happy.

They defined success that helps others and at the same time makes you feel happy. If you want a meaningful job you must have 2 conditions present, the ability to do your best and be challenged by what you do to provide something meaningful.

The fledgling business, Sony described it so well when they began with their initial purpose statement. "to establish a place of work where engineers can feel the joy of technological innovation, be aware of their mission to society, and work to their hearts content"

This is a brilliant example of how flow enters the workplace.

For Flow to be present there are 7 conditions that must be present, and this is irrespective of age, religion or level of education.

They are.

1. The person must be completely involved in what they are doing – Focused and concentrated
2. A sense of ecstasy – Of being outside the everyday reality

3. Great sense of inner clarity – Knowing what needs to be done and how well we are doing it.
4. Knowing the activity is doable – that our skill level are adequate to the task even thought it may be difficult
5. A sense of serenity – no worries about oneself, and a feeling of growing beyond the boundaries of the ego
6. Timelessness – Thoroughly focused in the present, hours seem to pass by in minutes
7. Intrinsic motivation

Once these conditions are met the activity becomes worth doing for the task itself

He went on to measure, very accurately, the level of challenge and the level of skill people brought to a task and to discover how it affected their sense of flow.

He discovered that people have a set point. And if the challenge is higher than your set point or the skills you bring to it are higher than your set point he is able to predict very accurately when you enter this state of ecstasy of flow.

For most people this will be when you are doing what you really enjoy doing. Playing music in a band, sport, work, computer games or study.

He developed a scale which predicts reasonably accurately when someone might go into a flow experience (see diagram below)

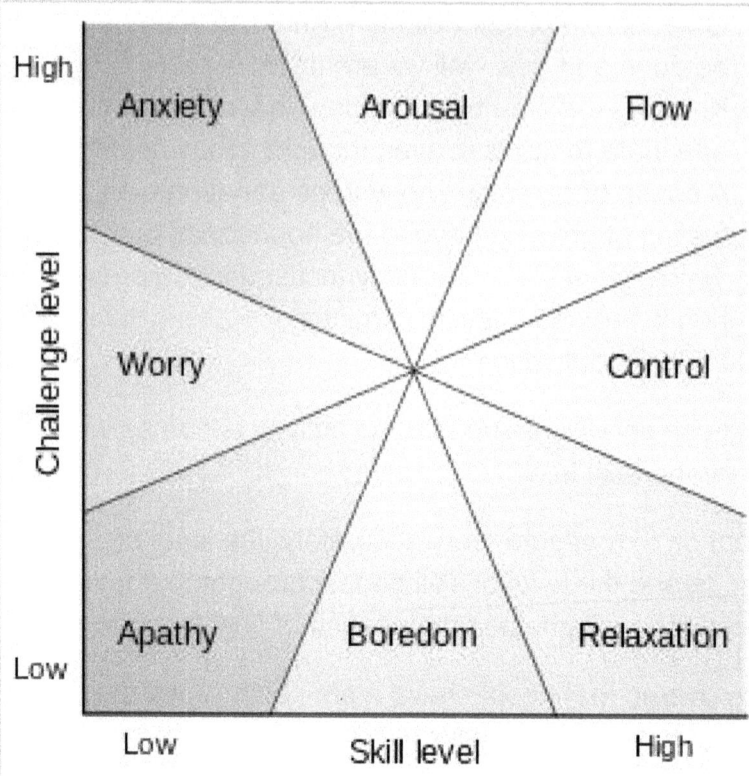

When someone is dealing with a task that requires skill level far below their set point or their level of challenge then they will drop into apathy or boredom. And this is a fairly awful state to be in. If you increase the level of challenge too much without providing the corresponding skills you will move into worry and anxiety. Many people experience this state of apathy while watching television which requires low skill and low challenge. It's a negative state to be in.

Most flow experiences start from the position of either arousal or control. An increase in the level of challenge beyond the comfort zone when you are in control will get you into flow. And an increase in skill from arousal will likewise get you to a flow state as well.

Control is comfortable but not very exciting, so it's a good place to enter flow from.

The real question is how can we put more and more of life into this flow channel. And in my little group the question was how to I keep my team in a state of flow for as much of the time as is possible.

Why would I want to do that. Because the more flow experiences you have in your day the higher you would rate your happiness according to Csikszentmihalyi.

One of the ways he suggests to move into the flow channel is to have a group of skilled teammates and increase the challenge level.

Encouraging flow in workplaces

Because flow is linked closely with achievement, its development could have a positive effect in increasing workplace satisfaction and accomplishment. Flow researchers, such as Csikszentmihalyi, believe that interventions may be useful to enhance and increase flow states in the workplace, through which people would gain 'intrinsic rewards that encourage persistence"

This certainly was what we experienced in our team. An increase in persistence and to a certain extent resilience was a great result of providing consistent challenges in an environment that was closely matched to the skills levels of our team mates. Often requiring a slight increase in the skill level to match the new challenge. So players were entering a flow state from both control and arousal state.

Other authors such as Coert Visser, furthers the ideas

presented by Csikszentmihalyi, with their integration into the workplace. He suggests that an ideal work place is one that an employee can both contribute something meaningful beyond themselves while using skills that are closely matched to their current inventory.

Your team will likely experience flow when they are doing their best work in a task that requires full involvement and focus and the skills for the task closely match one's ability.

Visser [21] in his book "Good Work" suggests that managers and business owners provide tools by which you can create an atmosphere that makes it easier to enter flow states and encourages greater levels of persistence in achieving tasks and happiness in your charges lives..
In order to achieve flow, Csikszentmihalyi says the following three conditions need to be present:

1. Clear goals
2. Immediate feedback
3. A balance between opportunity and capacity, or a balance between challenge and skills required

It appears that with increased experiences of flow, people experience "growth towards complexity," that is people flourish as their achievements grow and that comes with development of increasing emotional, cognitive, and social cohesiveness within a team environment.

Creating a workplace atmosphere that allows for flow and growth, Csikszentmihalyi argues, can increase the happiness and achievement of its team members as well.

Why wouldn't flow experiences occur at in a team?

One of the principal reasons is a lack of clear goals. Some people may not understand how their task fits into the bigger picture and having an absolutely clear understanding of how their effort contributes to the big plan would significantly increase commitment.

In many small to medium businesses the owner or directors often don't share their goals with their team, I assume only because of an attempt to keep control, and I see this contributing to significant disengagement amongst employees.

The second reason this wouldn't work is that feedback is limited and the team member is unaware of whether they are doing a good job or not. This is a significant contributor to demotivated employees.

When there is little communication of feedback, an employee may not be assigned tasks that challenge them or seem important, which could potentially prevent opportunities for flow. The less flow experiences an employee has the lower their level of happiness. The link appears to be that direct.

In her article in *Positive Psychology News Daily*, Kathryn Britton examines the importance of experiencing flow in the workplace beyond the individual benefits it creates. She writes, "Flow isn't just valuable to individuals; it also contributes to organizational goals. For example, frequent experiences of flow at work lead to higher productivity, innovation, and employee development (Csikszentmihalyi, 1991, 2004). So finding ways to increase the frequency of flow experiences can be one way for people to work together to increase the effectiveness of their workplaces." [#22]

Flow is an innately positive experience and studies have shown that it produces feeling of enjoyment, sometimes quite intense feelings. These feelings are so intense that they contribute positively toward happiness in the long term. Some have suggested that continual small improvements and wins create a sense of meaning, achievement and satisfaction. In other words happiness. The more you can engineer flow experiences into your teams works life the happier they will be. The more motivated, focused and productive they'll be.

Flow theory tends to imply continual growth, in that you must continually increase your skill and challenge to maintain flow experiences. You are focused intently on mastering increasingly greater skills.

Attempting these new, difficult challenges stretches your skills and you emerge from a flow experience with a bit of personal growth and great feelings of competence and mastery.

[21] *Visser, Coert. "Good Business: Leadership, Flow, and the Making of Meaning". Retrieved 26 September 2012.*

[22] *Britton, Kathryn (7 September 2008). "Flowing Together". Positive Psychology News Daily.*

Chapter 7
ADAPT AND CHANGE

Why is transition so important?

The concept of transition is all about how quickly you can change and adapt your behaviour from one state to another. And I believe it's ramifications are far greater than just the soccer pitch.

Every team has setbacks, it's just part of the game, but I believe that the quicker you can transition from a setback to a more resourceful mode of behaviour the quicker you'll win the game.

And I'm not just talking about soccer. I'm talking about personal states, business, families, musicians, politicians... everyone.

Transition is a core value that has had great effect on the field and in business.

Just acknowledging that there will be a constant change of ball possession, or a constant change from attack to defense changes the way I think about teams.

How Transition relates to your work teams and your business.

I believe that games are a reflection of life. How we play a game is a direct reflection of how we deal with our lives and in many cases our businesses.

Why is it that sports people are so good at business. Look at legendary rugby players, John Eales and Nick Farr-Jones. Great leaders, brilliant sportsmen and very successful at business.

The concept of transition in sporting teams relates to how you move from a defensive phase of play to an offensive or attacking phase. Or the other way around.

in a game of Soccer/football even the most dominant teams will only have possession, or be in the positive or attacking phase of play for 60% of the time. What that means is that everyone will be dealing with defensive play for a fair portion of the game.

Defensive phase

In business we are all dealing with attack after attack and we feel that we are in a defensive mode, repelling the bombardment of

But how do we then transition into attack.

What does this look and sound like for a business owner. Not enough time, moving office, tax problems, not enough money, can't get started on anything to move forward.

It's not unlike a team that is sustaining attack after attack and they are defending their goal. They are limiting their liability or loss. The common offensive structure for a team is to become compact and compress. we do that in business by downsizing, getting rid of excess staff, containing costs, moving to a smaller office etc.

In sporting teams this is about defending the goal and everyone gets behind the ball to repel the attack.

When you are playing a brilliant opponent you are often repelling wave after wave of attack. And yet some of the most brilliant players are defensive minded. In fact if you don't have a well-organized center defensive team within your team then you are going down.

The elements to great defense are the ability to scramble and react to new situations while remaining organized, the ability to know where your team mates are and how to use them to the best effect. Strong Leadership, supporting your team mates and a willingness to put yourself on the line to defend.

Lucas Neil, the former captain of the Socceroo's, is one of the great defensive players our country has produced. He is constantly alert, never ever gives up on his job, he is a leader and leads by example, he trains relentlessly and constantly acquire new skills by playing in different leagues.

He is organized, disciplined and equal parts nurturing and creating high expectations for his team mates and holds them accountable to achieving them.

When under attack he does not panic but knows what his job is. He organizes those around him while he is also doing his own job.

So transition out of defense is already in the mind of the payers while they are defending.

What does Transition out of a defensive phase look like in business?

Traditionally it is reducing costs and unnecessary resources such as staff and office space.

The attacks that business owners usually sustain are losing a major client or cash flow issues, or dwindling demand for your services. Team problems are another attack, needing to bring in new clients is often the main strategy for moving out of defense. Transition is perceived to be taking place when more work comes in the door. But is that the definition of transition.

In sport once a team has the opportunity

And once they have the advantage to move out of a defensive phase of play. Whether that is by a fast counter attack to take advantage of a disorganized opponent or by maintaining possession of the ball while his offensive players move to an advantageous position. Either way they are thinking about the attacking phase almost before they are finished with the defense.

In fact when they are right in the most intense part of defending the attack they are prepared for the transition. If they react with a knee jerk response this will likely prolong the defensive phase

For example. If our defenders just kicked the crap out of the ball and put it back into the opponents half that would momentarily relive the attack. However the other team would simply control the ball and within seconds you would be defending again.

If however we could gain control of the ball and maintain possession by passing to team mates that are not under pressure from opposition, then the opposition is suddenly chasing the ball.

And if Lucas Neil's team can be more organized than the opposition then they can make their opponents run around chasing the ball while his attackers get into positions where they don't have any pressure. Moving into space where you can make a creative decision about how you choose to attack the goal.

9 tips for transitioning your work team out of a defensive phase of business

1. Get help. No one can move out of a defensive position all by the self. It takes a team. In business that means talk to people who can help you. Talk to people that have an understanding not only of where you are now and where you want to be, but people that help you with strategies that set you up for the transition to the future. It takes differing strengths to be able to deal with different aspects of defense. Sometimes you'll need muscle and strength, sometimes you'll need calm decision making, other times you'll need to consolidate and make the easy and safe first step.

2. Practice, prepare and then practice some more. Can sports professionals practice too much for a big game? Not likely. Why then do we not practice and rehearse for the next phase of our businesses. How can you practice? Read a book a week - Jim Rohn, don't wish things were easier... wish you were better.

Set goals and plan strategies that will get you there. E.g. How will you fund the growth, what will your organizational chart look like, who do you need to hire first, what additional skills do you need.

3. Counter attack. Take advantage of a weak opponent or a gap in the market place or an opportunity. But so it fast. And know what your plan is before you count attack. Just running ahead without organization and pre planning to take into account the conditions you are attacking into will not result in a victory

4. Look inward first. Look at the strengths of your team and how they can be strengthened and prepared for the transition, are the roles they are in best suited for the job.

5. Play a safe move first. Most business owners feel that the only way to get out of a defensive position is to get more clients. New clients = cash flow problems go away. So they will often spend lots of money on marketing, advertising, brochures or online campaigns without testing and measuring to make Certain you are not throwing money away. This can be the equivalent of kicking the ball to apparent safety only to have it come back to you almost immediately

6. You will need to make the right decisions and make them really quickly. the wrong decision will put you Straight back to a defending again. Define the parameters of what a good decision looks like.

7. Communication within your team is vital. That's not just your employees, if you are a one person business your team includes your business advisors such as your accountant, your solicitor, your network, your coach and even your suppliers. Everyone needs to know the short term goals and what the expectations

are in order to get there. Having a common goal at this phase of business is critical.

8. Complaining about a decision that you feel the referee has made or a foul by the opposition just takes your eye off the process of transition. W saw that in the Manchester game on the weekend. The all starts were so busy appealing to t he referee that the player was offside that they didn't concentrate on nullifying the threat.

9. Do the business basics well and be efficient with them. Learn to have mastery over the basic elements of your business. Your product and service needs to be not just good, but brilliant, every time. Your Customer service needs to be great... and consistent. Your financial management and understanding of key performance indicators in your business must be sound.(this doesn't mean that your finances need to be in good shape because in the defensive phase of business they are often not good at all. What it means is that you know what the indicators mean for your business, things such as cash flow gap, break even point and margins, know what your conversion rate is and learn to measure everything)

Chapter 8

IF YOU DON'T UNDERSTAND PEOPLE YOU DON'T UNDERSTAND TEAMS.. OR BUISNESS

I find it curious that many people who are put in charge of team don't really seem to either like people or be interested in what makes them behave the way they do.

It seems that in many organizations where someone is a brilliant technician, perhaps a lawyer or engineer or IT guru, and they have been in one place long enough the powers to be decide to make them a manager or team leader. And how well does that work out most of the time?

I hear team members say their boss doesn't help them, communicate with them in anything other than moody tantrums or worse.... their bosses are indifferent to them.... they just don't seem to give a crap about supporting their team mates, or they do just enough to keep HR off their backs.

Indifference is the Killer of teams....

Actually, Indifference is the killer of people.

You can handle an interaction at either end go the spectrum. If someone doesn't like you or is openly hostile to you, you have some choices to make, it will fire you up to action. You will want to prove them wrong, or right or anything just to stick it to them… You are in a state of motivation. You may not like it and it may not be comfortable but you are moving forward.

If someone is totally supportive of you then you feel like you can take risks, you feel like you are invincible and that you can take on the world. Again you are motivated into action. If someone really believes in what you are doing and supports you 100% then just sitting on your hands doing nothing just seems like you are letting the team down and you are motivated.

But indifference…. That's a killer….. Of people's spirits and of your team.

So if you are a team leader of any sort. A work team, family unit or a sporting or community team then you MUST NOT BE INDIFFERENT. Because if you are then you have chose to slowly kill off the spirit of the people you have been charged with leading.

And that's worse than being a bad boss. In my opinion the definition if evil is when someone actively works to kill off the spirit of another human being.

You are put in Charge…. So lead.

Get to know what motivates your team, start to understand how human behavior is motivated and expressed. because I promise you that if you don't understand people then you don't understand teams.

I'd take it further actually... I believe that if you don't understand people then you don't understand business.

I'd like to introduce you to what I consider a very practical way to understand your team members and the people behind the actions you see on the field. The DISC behavioural model.

DISC Explanation

The DISC behavioural is a system designed by the American Psychologist Dr. William Moulton Marsden. It places people into one of four different Behavioral types;

>D – Dominant,
>
>I – Influential,
>
>S – Steady and
>
>C – Compliant.

What I especially like about the DISC model is that it's not an airy fairy personality profile that is difficult to understand. It's practical and easily adapted by even the most casual observer. What's more it can and does help you understand those people you interact with frequently.

I also like it because it is an inclusive model and encourages difference in your team to be used for it's strengths. So it includes everyone, and no type is better or worse.

I find this system an immensely practical tool when dealing with clients and team mates. It explains the behaviours of people and therefore helps me understand how I can communicate an idea to them in the best possible way.

I use it at work especially when I need to build rapport with someone quickly, such as in a sales situation.

When I need to get a client into action I will be far more effective at that if I can communicate to them in a language that is in their Zone.

The DISC profile gives me a good understanding of their behaviours. They call it a personality assessment but in reality it's a model of observable behaviour.
And being able to speak another persons language builds deep rapport quickly.

Why are soft skills so important?

Many people I work with, especially high level technicians, suggest that they don't really need to understand or study people this deeply.

They may be an accountant and only want to work with numbers, or an analyst and be totally content with looking at screens all day, never having to connect with another person face to face. But it's now that I repeat. If you don't understand people you don't understand teams and you certainly don't understand business.

It doesn't matter whether you work with small or large teams, whether you are an employee in a multi-national or run a small Mum & Dad business. Very few people achieve anything all on their own. most people who achieve something do so with a team.

Even my computer game addicted son cannot compete in his online games without the help of teammates. So get to know how to understand why they do what they do and you will begin to have a level of mastery over your environment that you have never had previously

What does DISC measure?

The DISC profile measures people in four quadrants and uses 2 Axis. The vertical axis has at the top Outgoing people. That was once described to me as people who talk before they think. And at a the bottom of the vertical axis are reserved people. Those are the people who filter everything they say though their brain so it comes out just right.

Then there is the horizontal Axis. On the left are Task oriented people and on the right are People oriented people.

- If you are someone who is outgoing and people oriented we'd describe you as a high I
- If you are Outgoing and Task oriented we'd describe you as a high D
- If you are Reserved and People oriented then we'd say you are a high S, and
- If you are Reserved and Task oriented then we'd say you are a high C

See the image below

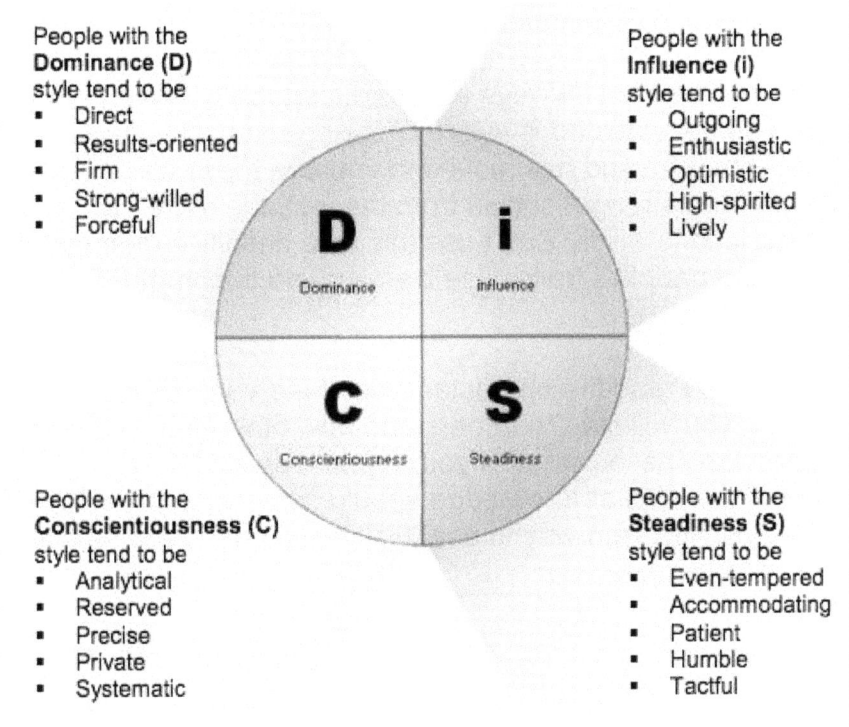

People with the **Dominance (D)** style tend to be
- Direct
- Results-oriented
- Firm
- Strong-willed
- Forceful

People with the **Influence (i)** style tend to be
- Outgoing
- Enthusiastic
- Optimistic
- High-spirited
- Lively

People with the **Conscientiousness (C)** style tend to be
- Analytical
- Reserved
- Precise
- Private
- Systematic

People with the **Steadiness (S)** style tend to be
- Even-tempered
- Accommodating
- Patient
- Humble
- Tactful

General DISC Theory

The DISC personality profile is an accurate personality analysis that can be used to predict the behaviour of individuals when they work on their own and with others. It can help you to place the right person in your business or on your team, working in an environment that suits both you and them.

However, this system is not infallible. Like anything, it has its limitations. Its shortfall is that people seldom have just one style. They are rather a combination of the four, just in different ratios. Everyone is dominant in one personality type, but another may be closely following.

The DISC test highlights a person's relative strengths in each of the four areas. The area that scores highest will be the person's dominant trait.

The results aren't always accurate, especially when the person being tested is aware of their personality eccentricities and has moved to improve these traits. The higher the strength shown from the test, the more the descriptions will fit. Don't use this as a definitive method for labeling people's traits. Use it as a guide to communicating with them.

When you read the characteristics of the various personality types, you will start to understand how other people see you when they associate with you. Again, this isn't always 100% accurate. With all knowledge should come wisdom. Knowing the best time and way to use this knowledge is what makes the difference.

DISC Under Pressure

When we measure your DISC profile we are looking at how you operate within your environment, Whether that's at work or within a team. We measure your natural style and your adapted style.

One way to understand this is to look at how typical styles operate under pressure.

Often a person stays the same under pressure. A High D can stay a High D. A High S can stay a High S and so on..

People can change their behavioural style under pressure. A High I can become a High S under pressure. This means the person slows down and thinks more; they become more reserved.

A High I can become a High D, which means instead of being friendly to everyone, they start to bossing everyone around without much regard to their feelings. People around them would wonder what happened to that friendly person that got on with everyone so well.

A High D can become to a High C under pressure. They will now consider details more and think carefully before making a decision. A High D could go to a High S, meaning they will steady themselves and slow down. They will consider the people around them more.

A High S could even become a High D under pressure. They now have to act and think quickly when placed under lots of pressure. They might start to become loud and bark out orders when normally they are calm, reserved and friendly.

A High C could move to a High D under pressure. They will think and act quicker than previously, making decisions quickly and not considering all the details. You've heard people say they work best under pressure; this could mean they've become a High D under pressure to get more done.

Normally a High C wouldn't change to a High I or High S under pressure, or a High I wouldn't go to a High C under pressure, as these two personality types are so different.

It is really important to understand the different behavioural styles of your team. Why? so you can speak their language when you need to.

If one of the team mates is a high C and under pressure become a high D then I'll need to know how to communicate in a very fast effective way to keep the team on track. And in a sports team I only have about 10 minutes at half time to do that for each of the individual players and reorient them back to what working and what needs to be better.

One of my U/16's was a classic at transforming, and putting off his team mates, with his behavioural style. And it needed to be handled. He is a high C, extremely intelligent, and absolutely on task. He has very, very little people orientation or empathy in him.

Both High C and high D are very task oriented and expressing the job at hand to him quickly and in a logical manner would be highly effective. However the High C that turns to a high D under pressure would likely say everything that comes into their head no matter what. Which usually means some hurt feelings from their teammates. High D's are great because they love to take big risks, however I like to say they don't speak "people" very well

Like a bull in a China Shop

When things get really pressured this player turned from a reserved high C to a very outspoken high D, telling everyone that would listen exactly what they were doing wrong and what they must do to correct it, in no uncertain terms. Often counteracting my instructions.

Sometimes players would come off in tears because he had said something quite hurtful in their eyes. And in truth most high D's have very little understanding of how what they say affects others. One of my team mates will say to me… Toughen up Princess and be completely oblivious to the potential hurt feelings that may accompany the comment.

How to manage that? Talk firmly, quickly and with absolute clarity, no fluffy language, High D's and High C's just don't understand it. Ask them pointed and direct questions that help them understand and ask them to make a decision.

Example
Coach: What did I ask you to do when the ball came out to you after a goal kick?

Player: You asked me to take it wide and pass it off up the line very quickly if I was shut down by the opposition. One touch if possible, and if unopposed to carry it as far as I could before offloading it and continuing the run.

Coach: How come you've been holding it for 3-4 touches?

Player: Not sure

Coach: What do you need for that to happen?

Player: I need the midfielders to come in and give me options.

Coach: Would it make a difference if you lifted your head early, prior to receiving the ball?

Player: Yes

Brett: Are you willing to give that a go?

Player: Yes.

Coach: Great, show me.

You also need to Establish that you are in charge and exactly what the instructions are, and you'll need to do that in far more detail than you would for someone that is a high I.

I would also appoint a strong leader on the field who every player would be respectful of. And make certain that the leader is operating on the same wavelength as I am.

We'll talk much more about the different personalities in the team and how to manage them in your own team, but from the moment I want to give you a more in-depth but practical look and different behavioural styles and how you can manage them.

First by recognizing your own style and then understanding how that style interacts with others.

For example I'm a high I with a fair bit of D in me too. That means when my team mate says something a little harsh to me I take it to heart a little more than I should. And I'm probably a little too verbose for some of my team mates, too chatty and probably too feelings oriented. I'm also married to a high D. Which makes life very interesting.

My wife is a brilliant, intelligent, beautiful high D. She knows what she thinks, is absolutely firm in her beliefs, (nearly black and white) and has always said that if she didn't have a man in her life that was equally as strong she would just walk all over them.

Her men need to have a strong spine. And after 29 years of marriage I can tell you she is right. I on the other hand am quite emotional and more feelings oriented. I've always been astute to the vibe in the air of a room or the unsaid communication between others, and I can pick up on human interactions from a distance whether they are good, bad or otherwise. I'm an outgoing people oriented person.

People fascinate me, and if you ask me a question I'll likely talk to you for much longer than you'd have liked. I'm outgoing.

So when my wife tells me something in a really blunt way I'll build meaning behind it and sometimes take it to heart just a little bit too much. She is the ultimate "toughen up princess" I'm the romantic one and she is the practical one. She sees things in black and white and I see millions of tomes of grey in-between. In many ways we are polar opposites. And it's not that long ago that she finally said to me.. Give me one of those bloody DISC things, I want to know which one I cam….. (I should have guessed straight away that she was a high D) and we did the score on her.

The fact that I now understood her behavioural style was of unimaginable comfort to me. I would regularly say to myself. Oh I get it… that's just you interpreting the world as a high D. In black and white. It's not my job to change the way you think about stuff, just to understand that's the way your brain works. And If I want to communicate with you then I would be far better served if I could do it in the style you understand best.

Of course it's a little more challenging for a high D to understand the infinite greys that I perceive but she does so in her own way. She has now come to refer to me as the girl in our relationship… the romantic one. And she makes many concessions to that.

If you don't understand people then you won't be as successful as you might otherwise be.

Here is a little more information about the different styles

The High I behavioural style

High I's like to have fun and be popular. You can recognize them by their outgoing and very friendly manner. They want to be people's friends. They will rarely tell anyone off. When they say something in anger, they don't want you to remind them of it again because that was in the past and they really weren't that serious when they said it in the first place.

High I's don't like to get into too much detail as they don't find that fun. They like to work with others in a changing environment. High I's can be recognized by their very friendly disposition. They look you in the eye and usually use a lot of tonal changes in their voice.

They talk a bit louder than other personality types, except

the High D who can also talk confidently and loud. This is the mark of an extrovert. The difference between them is that High I's are loud and friendly. If you joke with either of them, a High I will respond but a High D may not.

A High I will respond quicker because they think you're like them, so they'll let you know by giving you a friendly response.

High I Employees

They make good salespeople and get on well with people. However, they can be too friendly and this may annoy people as well. It especially annoys the High D's. A High I prefers to work with others and have a bit of fun.

Don't try to stop them from enjoying themselves though, or they won't hang around long. Let them be a team leader (unless there is a High D in the group who will sabotage the High I's authority).

High I's are good motivators because people will usually want to do what they ask as they are well liked.

High I Interaction

High I's get on fairly well with most personality types. They can annoy the High C and High D because they're task-orientated and just want to get the job done without being friendly while doing it. All the other personality types can see a High I as overly friendly. They might say, "Mellow out a bit. You come on too strong and annoy people. Don't be so friendly."

High I's are good motivators and team leaders although they won't like pulling a team member into line if they've done something they shouldn't have.

High I leaders

As a leader they will probably want to do what is popular. They can put up with people for too long without really telling them to get into shape.

They like to do new things. However, this won't appeal to them unless a few people tell them to do it and it seems popular. Their personality can cause them challenges in managerial positions because they won't want to put people off or make changes that will make them unpopular with other team members.

Persuading A High I

To persuade a High I you need to win them over and be their friend. If you don't show you care about them or that you like them, they won't want to buy whatever you are selling.

You need to show you have a sense of humour, are a fun-loving person and you are having fun talking to them right now. You can work on being a little bit stern but not too serious.

High I's want to do what seems popular. They don't want to do anything that seems like detailed work that will take up lots of their time. If it seems boring to them, they won't want it. The best thing you can say to them is It will be a lot of fun.

They will buy from people who seem to have the same nature as they do. So be happy and spontaneous. Talk about other things apart from what you are selling them. Get chatty at the start, during the middle and the end of the selling process. They will sometimes want to go off on a tangent.

Let them do most of the talking. They love to talk about anything, especially other people.

Be their friend and advise them on what you think and feel is best for them. Be sincere. Be like them and they will love you.

If you're a High D, don't talk too much. Let them decide they want it and that it seems like a popular idea and makes sense. High D's need to be friendlier than they usually are when selling to them.

You can't be too friendly with a High I – as long as you're sincere. They are people's people and have great people skills. They won't like you if you are fake.

High I's are prone to exaggerate. They like to tell stories and you can too when selling to them. But tell them if you are exaggerating.

Areas To Work On

High I's need to work on getting the job done and not being distracted by other people. They need to be more task-orientated. They need to get into the details more as this is what they don't like doing.

They need to be less extroverted with people, especially High C's and High S's. When communicating with a High C they don't need to be their friend, a belief that is hard to overcome for a high I

High I's are a bit too friendly for the High S, although the High S can see that aspect of them and not let it bother them. High I's need to recognize the other personality types are not like them. They also need to work on being more like the others when communicating with them.

High D Personalities

High D's like to be in control. They want to be at the top and give the orders. They have a hard time following orders as they feel their own way is always better. High D's will usually end up in managing positions, self-employed or in charge of a section that has a bit of room to move unsupervised.

They like to be in control of their own lives and make their own decisions. High D's can seem too powerful or strong for other people. They are confident, outspoken, and say what they feel. This can offend others, as they can be thought of as arrogant. They aren't usually; it's just the way they express themselves.

As High D's have active minds that like to be stimulated, they like to be doing lots of things at once. When they do more than one thing at a time, the quality can start to drop. It can be difficult for them to follow something to its end. They feel a great need for lots of activity. When you want something done in a hurry, give it to a High D.

High D Employees

High D employees like to be given responsibility and work best on their own. They like to have control. They aren't keen on taking orders continually.

They prefer to be given an outline of how to be productive and what's expected of them, then left alone to accomplish it. They won't come back asking for the details on how to do something. When given a task to do with others they will assume the leader's role. They feel they need to take on this role mainly because they feel more confident in their own abilities than other people's.

They always prefer to lead than to follow. They prefer to work on their own or to delegate tasks to others. They start a lot of things and usually don't finish them. They can start without really knowing where they are headed because they aren't great planners or thinkers. They just want to get in and do it.

They work well with High C's because they are the ones to delegate to.

High D's can sabotage authority because they don't like being given orders; they much prefer to give them. They will always feel they should be in control, making the decisions.

High D's are generally confident people because they have always been used to making their own quick decisions.

High D Interaction

A High D does not interact well with others. They give orders and like to take control and this can detract from their relationships with others.

A High D can sabotage or undermine the authority of a High I and not be at all worried about it affecting their popularity. While the High I likes to have fun working with a group, the High D isn't interested, or at least not to the same degree.

Often a High D has a lot of High I in them; they just need to tap into it more to get on better with a High I.

A High D works well with a High C. Neither needs to be friendly while they work, so they get the job done. The two personalities compliment each other very well. The High D gets on best with a High C. A High D likes to delegate, and the best one to delegate to is the High C.

However, because the High D is not detail-orientated and the High C is, a problem can occur. The High C will need lots of details on how to do something, and this is precisely something the High D doesn't like to give.

Also a High C prefers to do the same thing over and over. They like doing what they know how to do. That's often how they get their significance and feelings of importance; by doing something perfectly.

A High D gets along reasonable well with and a High S because the latter is steadying, reserved and tolerant of others. A High S doesn't need to be given the details like a high C does. They can just be told what to do and they do it.

A High S knows the High D likes to control others and doesn't let it worry them. A High D doesn't consider their mode of interaction, like needing to relay instructions with details for the High C, or with friendliness to a High I, so the High S works best with a High D.

A High D may think the High S is inferior, because they mistake their natural reserve and steadiness with lacking in confidence. Often a High S has great self-confidence; they just don't need to display it like a High D does. High D's like confident people as they can relate better to them.

High D Leaders

They can often be found being busy. They want to achieve, produce, get lots done, and work hard and long hours to succeed. Sometimes they just don't stop to look and see if they are really producing or achieving anything. They don't slow down long enough to see if they are making progress.

This isn't true of every High D but many are like this at some level. In leadership they often don't finish things. They like to be doing lots of things at once because their minds are active and they need to stay active. They can delegate but often don't follow-up to see if standards are met.

They aren't perfectionists unless they have a strong High C

influence in their personality. They like to do a lot quickly, which sums them up fairly well.

They can make good managers, as they prefer to be told what results are expected of them and then left alone to get on with the job. If a High C is giving them orders, they will get irritated and bored, as the High C will want to monitor their progress and give them lots of instructions on how to do it.

A High D will often get started on a project before you finish telling them what it is. There are more multi-millionaires that are High D than any other personality type, mainly because they get in and have a go and just try something. And they keep on trying with great effect. They also don't try to do everything on their own. They delegate.

Persuading A High D

High D's like to be leaders. They like to do what no one else is doing. They like to be innovative pioneers. The best way to persuade them is to tell them what they need to be more productive, profitable, successful and a leader of others.

Respect them and never make them feel inferior. They need to respect the person attempting to persuade them. Most importantly, they need to be confident you can deliver what you say you can. They need to be given the facts and reasons. Also, don't try and be too friendly with them.

They want a summary of any features. They don't need details; in fact going over details annoys them. Give a brief outline of different things showing the logic of it all. They want to be productive so tell them what you have will help that cause. Tell them they will be more successful using your service or item. That's what they want to know.

Give them better solutions or ways of doing things. Be blunt if you have to; they don't mind too much and they don't care

– but only if they have your respect.

Areas They Need To Work On

The major area they need to work on is their people skills and communication with others. They also need to slow down to check if they are making progress. When talking to a High C, they need to give more specifics.

They need to be friendlier to others they work with. They need to have a checking system on their progress and of how well they are doing. Are the jobs they start being completed, and if so, how good is the quality? They need to stop, plan and think more before they start, and also as they progress.

High S Personalities

High S's are steady people. They don't like to rush things. When everyone else is stressing out, they remain calm. They like to plod along, thinking things over before doing anything. They don't like making quick decisions.

They are well liked by all personality types because they are friendly easy-going and harmless. People admire their cool disposition. They just get in and get the job done, although usually not at a great pace.

While the High D starts, going flat out without knowing if they are doing it right, the High I gets everyone together so they can all get involved and have fun.

The High C plans every detail meticulously before making a start, while the High S is thinks it over before making a slow start.

High S As Employees

They are good team players. You can get them to do anything, and they are happy doing it. They prefer to work with others but don't really care if they are on their own. They are the personality types you often can't figure out.

They aren't as forward as the High I, but they are definitely friendly. You'll see that in their eyes. While the High C will hold eye contact, their gaze isn't with the same interest and warmth as that of the High S.

They laugh easily and like to be with people. They make great sales people but usually only if they are already attracted to selling. They have a natural ability to build good rapport. High S isn't critical of other people like the High C or High D can be, or if they are, they don't tell everyone.

If you need a sales person, a High S can be very good, but only if they want to be a sales person. They have a real challenge with selling if they aren't already in sales. They often feel like they are being unfriendly by asking people to buy or by using closing lines. It is very hard for them to change this attitude as they resist all changes in their lives. Change comes to them slowly and steadily and usually only when there is very good reason. A High D will change in a blink compared to a High S.

High S Interaction

High S's get on well with High D's because they probably understand them and it doesn't worry them when the High D gives orders. Because the High S is calm, they are a help to the High D.

A High S can plan things, which is a help to the High D. They slow the High D down, and this can be both a good thing and a bad. High D's often end up marrying High S's.

The High S gets along well with the High I. They are both people-orientated. The High S is a calmer, more reserved version of the High I. The High S might say to the High I, "Mellow out. You come on too strong. You're too friendly." While the High I will respond, "Get a bit more life in you."

They both have fun in life, or try to. The High S has a high concern for others and tries to understand them. When a High I works with a High S, they can often get carried away with having fun, as they're not as task-orientated as the High D and High C.

The two usually won't get as much done as the other two personality types.

High S and High C are both introverted. They both like to take their time in making a decision. They work well together, although they won't get a task done as quickly as the D's and I's. They will think about it for a while first.

The High S will feel there's no need to rush into it. The High C will agree because they will want to consider all the details before they start anyway. The High C will be planning it out perfectly before they start, and if it's taking too long to start, the High S won't say too much because they like to keep the peace.

However the two personality types will get a job done well together and it will be done correctly.

The High D and High S get a job done well and complement each other nicely. The High S will bring the High D's feet back down to earth and steady them. The High D will speed up the High S's decision-making process, which is sometimes needed.

The High S admires the High D's leadership ability, while the High D admires the High S's steadiness – although not always. Because the High S is reserved while the High D is outgoing, they learn from each other in different situations.

High S Leaders

High S leaders will often plod along, not making drastic changes, doing what they know. They prefer not to rush anything. They don't make quick decisions. They feel there is rarely any need to rush things.

The High S will like to take time getting around to doing anything. They have their own steady pace. They can get in and work hard just like anyone else, as long as they don't have to make any major decisions or do anything that requires them to change personally.

The High S likes to work with others and usually considers their view. They are a team player and like to have a good working atmosphere. They will often employ other High S's, High C's and High I's. However, a High D can get on their nerves sometimes, because they like to make quick decisions and get some action happening. This is something the High S often isn't keen on.

There can be a clash of interests with a High D as these two are opposites. It is extremely rare to find a High S-D personality due to their major differences. One is introverted and other isn't. One is task-orientated and the other is people-orientated.

A High S can employ a High D to their benefit as a team leader when they need a person who can take control. In cases like this, they will be an asset. A High S likes to keep the peace and get on well with everyone. This can stop them from putting people off, keeping them on longer than is necessary, or being tolerable to others.

Persuading A High S.

They are harder to persuade to than the High D or I. They like to be steady in their decision-making. They don't like to rush anything – they like to take their time in reaching a decision. They don't like pressure or pushy people.

You need to be their friend and build genuine rapport with them. Be reserved like they are. Be casual. Outline what you want them to do, then give details. Give them data to make a decision and tell them they need to make it soon.

Don't expect quick decisions, though. Explain at the start if you can give them everything they want and expect today, and you both agree it's the best thing, then you'll outline the steps needed to get the process under way. Then ask if it's OK to do that? Get them to commit to making a decision there and then if you can.

Sometimes a High S won't make a decision at all on the day. If that's the case, be aware it often happens. Give them some time and get back to them the next day. Be firm in wanting a decision soon (or today) but don't be pushy.

Be reserved like they are. The High S doesn't like change, so tell them your product won't involve any major changes. Tell them it's a nice slow process.

Give them plenty of eye contact. Build rapport and be their friend.

Areas For A High S To Work On

The High S needs to work on changing their ways quicker. They change in time, however they are the most reluctant of all personality types to do so. A High D will change before you finish telling them why they need to. To a High I change is fun. They like change because they like variety in their life.

A High C won't usually change much at all. This is because they have just finished learning how to do something the best way they can and now they just want to keep doing it. They love getting into a routine and staying that way. How can you achieve perfection in anything if you don't stick to it for ages?

High S's need to practice making quick decisions and not looking back once they've made the decision. They need to realize often a quick decision is better than no decision at all.

High C Personalities

The High C is interesting in many ways. They have a tendency to collect data, facts and figures. They can often stutter their words when describing things, possibly due to tension and also because they are thinking what the perfect way to describe this is. High C's often stutter more than other personality types.

High C's like to do things very well, if not perfectly. However, they don't reference their standards to others, which would be valuable to them because then they would learn that their standards are much higher than everyone else's.

They often create stress in their lives by this ongoing striving to live up to their own perfect standards. They can miss out on seeing the big picture as they can get stuck on the details.

They want to work on their own because they feel they will do the job best. They think other people won't do as good a job as they will. A High C is reserved and task-orientated, which means they aren't that friendly in communication with other people, especially non-family and -friends.

They like to give lots of data when they communicate, as they feel this is what people want.

They can have high levels of stress due to rarely being able to live up to their own standards. They like to have many details before making a decision. They virtually never rush into anything, especially without considering all the facts, data and graphs. Then they like to think more on it.

They don't like to be pushed into doing things, as they feel their way is nearly always the best. They like to plan things out before lifting a finger. Conditions usually have to be perfect before they proceed.

High C Interaction

High C's complement a High D because they are virtual opposites; one is introverted and the other is extroverted. The High C is reserved while the High D is outgoing. Both are task-orientated.

The High C gets self-satisfaction and pride from doing things for others. Although if they don't know how to do what the High D is asking, there can be problems.

The High C needs to be shown in detail how to do something. The High D isn't into details, so a communication problem can occur. For this paring to work, the High D needs to explain in more detail how to do the things they want done.

A High C and High I are an interesting combination. They can work well together, although they can often have troubles. When they struggle in relationships, it can be due to their opposite nature. A High I is extroverted, while a High C is introverted.

A High I person is people-orientated while a High C is task-orientated. These traits can cause a lot of conflict. The High I will say or think that the High C is spending too much time on unimportant things. The High C may think the High I is airy-fairy and doesn't work on what is really important.

The High C will want the High I to be less friendly and more task-orientated, while the High I will think the opposite.

As a working combination, the two are good for each other if they can put aside their differences. The High I will stop the High C from being introverted and get them to have more fun and work with others. The High C will bring the High I back down to earth and get them working on the details. As a combination in business, they can work well together.

Persuading A High C

Persuading a High C can be challenging. A High C can be very skeptical of anyone who says they have something they'll need, because they often feel what they already have is good.

They can often resist change because they have their own way of doing things. They won't consider making a decision unless the facts are shown, are valid and there are lots of them.

Be prepared to spend a lot of time with them. They will ask a hundred questions and procrastinate, because they will be wondering whether they've covered every detail they need to know about.

They will be wary of sales people. This is mainly because they have found how to do things without anyone's help, and a new system will mean they'll need to re-learn. They're much happier doing what they already know how to do.

They aren't overly friendly like the High I and High S. You can't just tell them they need your item like you can the High D. They only want one thing; data. So give them as much data as you can. And give it in graph form, table from, written form, or essay from.

You can't give a High C too much data to consider. They like to justify their decisions by logic. They don't care if you are their best friend. They always consider the facts first.

Don't expect a High C to make a quick decision. They like time to think. So give it to them. Talk about facts backed by logic. Get back to them another day only if you tell them you've given them everything they need to make a decision.

They are confident in their own abilities and are used to making their own decisions. They will talk confidently because they have a lot of knowledge and are proud of it. If you tell them you have a way of helping them do things better and more efficiently, you will get their attention, and possibly the sale, eventually. Anything that improves their standards or efficiency they will love. Tell them you'll be able to do even better with this.

High C leaders

High C leaders can get themselves into stressful situations. They often want to do a lot of tasks themselves because they have higher standards that they feel always need to be adhered to. They feel they do things best so they should do everything.

The High C likes to make a better mousetrap and works on building a better one instead of marketing the one they already have. To them, perfection is the only way. They forget you can have the most valuable, efficient product in the world but without good selling and communication skills, they won't make a dollar.

The High C can get caught up with working on the appearance, perfecting the accounting system, or having the best and most efficient sales registers, yet none of these will really make them more money.

They can sometimes forget about finding out what the customer really wants because they are task-oriented. Most people in business do this, instead of finding out exactly what the customer wants, then selling that to them.

The High C can get caught up in doing the menial things in a business instead of working in it, dealing with customers and building a relationship. The High C needs to work more on relationships with their customers as well as their team.

The employee's happiness plays a major part in a business' success, and the High C can often forget to work on team building.

High C's need to work more with people and enjoy themselves. They should get in High S's and High I's or even High D's to improve things. A High I can help make them focus more on people and to have fun. A High D can help them be more productive and to get more things started each day.

Areas For The High C To Work On

Their own standards can be too high compared to others. They can be stressed people due to their feeling that everything they do needs to be perfect. This is the standard they always strive for. It can come from the fact they don't realize their standards are already far above anyone else's.

They need to get someone else's opinion when working on a task and accept their standards as being good enough. A High C needs to strive for excellence, not perfection!

Most High C's think they can do a better job and often they can. But usually the standard a High C works to is the minority's opinion because everyone else acknowledges excellence while a High C keeps on chasing perfection. High C's need to stop at excellence.

They need to work more with others to get used to their level of excellence, and then to accept it as their own 'new' standard.

A High C needs to be more confident in their approach to decision-making and not fear arriving at a wrong decision. After all, High D's make decisions a lot quicker than a High C ever will. And High D's far, far, outweigh High C's when it comes to successful people. So High C's need to get into the habit of making quicker decisions so they can develop better, stronger emotional muscle.

A High C needs to do things that are new or different. They need to forget their schedule. Throw it away for a day. Do something spontaneous. Do something on the spur of the moment. Do something because it looks like fun. They need to tell themselves change is fun; that it is good. They need to be more spontaneous.

They also need to get more help from others. They need to ask themselves if what they are doing is the most important thing they could be doing. Will spending the time doing it perfectly, really benefit them or others, or should they say, "This is excellent, what can I do next?"

High C's need to move on more quickly. They need to get more involved with people. They need to open up and tell others what they are feeling. A very wise man once said, "Vulnerability is strength because you open yourself up to change and improvement."

High C's need to be spontaneous more often. They need to take on more like a High D does. They need to do more things at once so they don't get stuck on the details which aren't always important.

Chapter 9

LEARNING TO LISTEN; PRACTICAL APPLICATIONS

How to use listening in your team

Playing above the line we recognize that if we listen to our team mates and understand what is really going on for them we will create trust at a significantly deeper level of trust and engagement.

And best of all you aren't relying on someone else to start this thing off. You can start it.

A W.I.F.L.E.

Not everyone has the ability to put aside their own feelings and do the reflective listening exercise, but nothing could be more important to the health of your team.

So we create a ritual for the team that allows everyone to have their say and feel heard.

There are many names for this ritual. In some circles they call it a WIFLE [What I feel Like Expressing], and in some native American Indian tribes they called it the talking stick.

When my wife and I were learning to listen we used the talking stick method and it worked very effectively.

It goes like this.

Whoever has the talking stick gets to express what they feel like saying, and everyone else gets to listen. Not comment, or refute or question. Just listen.

When that team member is finished they pass it onto the next person in the group and ask, what do you feel like expressing.

And so it goes around until everyone has had a chance to express how they are feeling.

The insights this shows the group is amazing. The feeling that each member of the group has a moment to really talk creates a vibrant energy. And it reveals all sorts of interesting and useful things to the group and particularly to the leader.

At this point they don't get to practice their reflective listening skills, but this is the beginning of the process. And it's a safe environment to start feeling heard.

At the end of the round I suggest that you give people in the group the opportunity to respond if they would like to. We sometimes call this a burning, as in I have a burning desire to talk about that issue so and so bought up.

I believe that in work groups especially this is vital to do as frequently as possible. For some that might be daily, weekly and others just at the beginning of each meeting.

The thing that this does is to give everyone a sense that what they have to contribute is important and it gives both the leader and each team member an insight into the state of mind of everyone at the table.

Many times I have done this with a work group and we've discovered that one of the group is having a tough day, or dealing with a personal issue that might be affecting their work. Once understood this dissipates much of the potential tension about their performance and the group can move into a more resourceful state.

Let me give you an example.
In one of my work groups one of the team members seemed particularly withdrawn and distracted, and when there is even one person in a group of 8-10 like that it has quite an effect on the entire team.

It was her time to talk and Irene kind of blew everyone off a little with a very flippant explanation of what she felt like sharing. Once everyone had their say it was time for anyone in the group to respond.

One of the directors of the company challenged her on what was going on and enquired about why she was withdrawing from the group so much. He was a little angry, frustrated but also concerned that his usually buoyant, vibrant extrovert was acting quite out of character. He couldn't sit on it any longer. I suspect this had been going on for a few days and could sense the frustration had been building.

He had a burning desire to find out what's going on and so he brought the issue to the group when everyone had finished.

She then revealed that she was undergoing a fairly serious medical procedure and frankly her prospects weren't looking too good. She was waiting on a transplant that didn't look like it was coming anytime soon. Understandably she had a raft of feelings about that and it was affecting her work, not to mention the rest of her life.

The group had been barely tolerating her withdrawn and slightly cynical persona that day, their reaction to her in this state was frustration. We were attempting to get an outcome in that meting after all.

Now, however, they understood what was going on underneath it all and it made sense to them. They had gained an deeper understanding of what was motivating the actions and reactions of their colleague.

Of even greater importance was that Irene had the opportunity to be heard, to let some of her colleagues into her world.

As soon as this happened the mood of the group changed. Now it all made sense and we could stop guessing as to why she was behaving this way. It wasn't about the topic we were talking about, she didn't have a problem with the task at hand, she had a mountain of other worries that just couldn't be contained anymore and she didn't have anyone to hear how she was feeling about that.

The team needed her to perform certain important functions within the group, we were relying on her. However now we could see the whole picture and I saw the group come together to create strategies for helping her both look after herself and her state of mind and keep up with her responsibilities to the group.

What I saw happen was the group coming together under pressure to support one of it's team mates through something very challenging.

I also saw something very human happen, I saw trust built to a much greater level and I saw the disordering of the old structure of ignoring personal challenges and their effects on the group. I also saw the reordering of the group into a new stronger structure better able to withstand increased pressures. And it all started with listening and understanding each other.

Now you may say to yourself that this is all very fluffy and nice and those of you who love to look at profits and balance sheets as the ultimate score sheet will be snorting in derision right now. If I can't measure it on a spread sheet then it's not really worthwhile giving it much attention.

Great, let's look at the P&L of this Group.

Once we stared to institute regular team meetings where we began by listening and understanding each other before getting into the tasks we needed to accomplish the profits rose. In fact they increased by about 20% over the next 4 months.

The amount of time the Director spent dealing with the team asking dumb questions dropped dramatically, falling to nearly zero within 9 months. Productivity of the team had increased by about 18%. And the director was able to spend a far greater amount of his time working on developing additional projects for the business to grow.

One senior staff member has left and as yet they have not needed to replace that position because of the efficiency gains in the remainder of the team (saving that team about $90K p/a in wages)

All up the fluffy stuff of team development, Increased trust through learning to listen and individuals taking ownership of their own development has seen this business add dramatic profits to the bottom line. And for the first time in a few years they showed a healthy profit.

Not very fluffy now is it. This is a small local business and I'd estimate that the owner will be pocketing at least an additional $350K this year because of the increased strength of his team.

Frequency of interaction – Arresting the slide back into old habits

It has been documented in many places that the frequency and quality of interaction within the group will have a massive impact on the productivity and performance of that groups output.

After a few months of working with the business I mentioned above it became apparent that the team were slipping back to old habits. People were feeling unsupported, others were not completing their tasks and customer complaints were on the rise.

My first question. How often are the team meeting?
Daily? Silence

Weekly? "Well we have our regular work in progress meetings"

O.K. Do you start those meeting off with the talking stick? How regularly are you doing listening to the state of mind of your teammates?

"We only do those every fortnight when we meet with you" they said a little sheepishly

Could you do a quick "What I feel like expressing" talking stick session every day? If you did how long would it take? Maybe only 3mins?

But we can't get the whole team together every day

Then what if you just did it with one other person, or just the two you work closest with. Would that make a difference.

The answer is yes. And not just because they went on to prove it so. Many studies show that frequent interaction between team mates increased the effectiveness of that team. When we started getting the critical people doing at least 3 quick stand up meetings that started with a talking stick the productivity increased

And recent studies are showing that face to face contact is by far the most effective form of contact. Electronic communication just isn't as effective.

Communication patterns are more important than talent

In his research published in the Harvard Business review in 2012 "the new science of building great teams" Alex "Sandy" Pentland showed this to be the case beyond doubt.

In this study researchers at MIT's Human Dynamics laboratory set out to solve the puzzle of why some teams consistently deliver high performance compared to other apparently identical teams.

They equipped 2500 people with wearable electronic sensors that collected data on their social behavior. They tested teams in banks, call centers and different businesses that handled customer service responsibilities.

They found with remarkable consistency that the most important predictor of a teams success was it's communication patterns. And those patterns were more influential than other factors such as intelligence, personality and talent combined.

Researchers could tell which teams would outperform by

looking at the data detailing the communication patters of its team mates.

They found that the best predictors of productivity were a team energy and engagement outside formal meetings. Those 2 factors explained approximately 1/3rd of the variations in profitability between groups. They measured the effect this had not just on the team's performance but on the dollar value to the business.

The data has revealed that successful teams share several defining characteristics.

1. Everyone on the team talks and listens in roughly equal measure. And contributions are short and sweet. Long soliloquies from managers to subordinates are not effective.
2. Members face one another and their conversations and gestures are energetic. Electronic communications such as email, texts and phone calls just won't achieve this.
3. Members connect directly with one another – Not just with the team leader. It clearly pays to encourage team mates to work together without a high level of hierarchical control so common on both sports coaches and dictatorial managers.
4. Members carry on back channel or side conversations within the team
5. Members periodically break, go exploring outside the team and bring information back. Keeping the idea of lifetime learning with a pluralist approach very much an important factor.

The data also showed something surprising. That individual reasoning and talent contribute far less than was expected. Implying that the best way to build a team is not to select members for their smarts, technical ability or accomplishments but to learn how they communicate and to shape and guild the team so that it follows successful communication patterns.

Without really knowing it this is exactly what I did with the All Saints team. I did not have the opportunity to select the team members. I inherited the team as they were. So instead I began to build trust, teach them what good communication looked like and how it affected their performance.

Pentland has identified three aspects of communication that contribute to a team's performance.

1. Energy
2. Engagement and
3. Exploration

Energy is the measure of the number and nature of exchanges amongst team members. An exchange can be as simple as a comment and an acknowledgement

The most valuable form of communication is Face-to-face and had the highest energy. Followed by phone or video conference as long as the numbers participating are not too great. They found that Phone and video conference gets less effective as more people participate

The least valuable forms of communication are email and texting.

Engagement reflects the distribution of energy amongst team members. Teams that have clusters of members who engage in high energy conversations and others who do not simply do not perform as well as teams where the distribution of engagement is more equal.

The third element of exploration involves members looking to outside engagements and connections with a view to bringing back fresh perspectives. Put simply the higher performing teams seek more outside connections. This is particularly important for creative teams and those responsible for innovation.

One challenge with his is that energy is a finite resource and spreading it too thin can be tricky. Engagement and Exploration don't easily co-exist. If team members devote more to their own team (engagement) and less to outside their team (exploration) their performance will be compromised.

Successful teams oscillate between the two and continue to do both. They Explore for discovery and engage for implementation of the ideas gathered from outside the group.

The Data that Pentland's team gathered was able to show with unprecedented accuracy that these 3 forces shape a team's performance.

For example. They found that the number of face-to-face exchanges between members accounts for 35% of the fluctuations in performance between teams.

They found that the right number of exchanges in a team is as many as dozens per working hour. But going beyond that decreases performance.
They also found that in a typical high performing team the members are listening or talking to the whole group only 50% of the time, and usually in short to-the-point statements. The other 50% of the time they are engaging in one-to-one conversations, which are usually quite short.

Traditional thinking says that these side exchanges distract from performance but the research shoes that it is a critical factor to higher performance.

Social time, it turns out, is critically important to team performance, often accounting for more than 50% of positive changes in communication patterns.

So providing structured socializing time within the framework of a group is vital. Rather than staggering meal breaks for work groups allow them to break together.

In one company increasing the size of the lunch tables allowed strangers to sit together and it improved performance dramatically.

Many organizations seek outside council when building a business case or doing a post mortem on a project. But the findings suggest that rather than only seek the same council over and over again the team would be better served from constantly seeking fresh perspectives from groups both within and outside the organization.

Within the soccer team I observed a small group of players that were energetic and engaged but only with their closest friends. It was a frustration that lost us many opportunities.

A small group of our players tended to pass the ball to their friends rather than make a pass to someone that was in a better position, the way teenagers so often do. It's behaviour deeply rooted in pack mentality and designed to increase their acceptance with the cool kids. But it's not very helpful for creating a high performing team.

What Pentland's research suggests is that if I can increase the one-to-one interactions between these players and others within the team that would be more resourceful for our performance then this might be a contributor to increased performance.

Chapter 10
WHAT HAPPENS WHEN THINGS DON'T GO AS PLANNED

The author Robert Kioyasaki once told a friend of mine - Never teach a pig to sing, it upsets the pig and drives you crazy.

Sometimes, people just don't want to know. And some certainly don't want to change. There are many, many people that are very happy to stay stuck in their old habits. Why? Because change is deeply un nerving for many people. The stress of giving up on old ways is so intense for some that it appears to be better to stick to old paradigms.

Unfortunately the progress and change that we are seeing, particularly in the workplace is increasing at such a rapid rate that we can no longer afford to ignore it. The old adage that if you aren't growing you are dying is more true in the modern workplace than at any time in history.

I had a few team members and their parents fairly consistently not act according to our team rules. And in every organisation I work in you will get people who do not want to change. You'll hear them say things like. "not this fluffy crap, I just want to get on with the job"

In our team we had players that were missing at training, late to games and despite not being 100% fit still wanted to play.

It's challenging in local soccer because some people just want to get their equal share of time on the field. You hear it from parents who clearly are working by a different set of rules to the rest of the team. "I've paid the same amount of money to play as everyone else on this team. I want my son to have equal time on the pitch." One parent hissed at me.

Well you and your son agreed to play by these rules and you guys were late to the game, we'd been underway for 10 minutes before you arrived at the field. Your son isn't prepared, warmed up on in a mental state of mind to play his best. When he is I'll get him on at the first opportunity.

What I really wanted to say was that if I put him on the field right now I would be letting the rest of the team down by putting someone on who was not ready. While the remainder of the team had arrived 45 minutes before the game, warmed up together, listened to the strategy I offered and sorted themselves out in preparation for a big game. You broke the rules and that means until you are fully ready to play as a part of this team then I'm not putting you on, and that might be half time because physical preparation is only part of the game.

Mental preparation and connection and team communication with the remainder o the team is what we'd been working on all season. In fact it's what has got us to the finals. And it might take some time at half time before that's established. It might mean that your son needs to sit on the sideline and study the game and where he can be most help before he is a fully functioning member of the team.

Which is what happened. His father was non too happy

about the fact that he didn't go on till so late in the game but that's the consequence for the action of being late and not living by the rules we had agreed to. When he went on however he was prepared and he contributed very nicely to the team's performance.

This particular team member was frequently late, and frequently not at training, and it was entirely out of his control. His parents were in charge of that. But it had an effect on the team. And he wasn't the only one.

It was a perfect example of giving 100% in order to get 100% Or only giving 50% and in return only getting 50%

If you ever wonder why people don't commit to you as much as you'd like them to just ask yourself, Am I committing to them as much as I could.

It seems to be a universal truth that you get as much as you are prepared to give. Another example of playing above the line... You are in charge of how much people commit to you. It starts with you.

This wasn't the only player on the team who didn't commit as much as others. One of our players didn't make the grand final because they had to work in a local shop at their part time work, I was told by their parents via email. The reaction from the remainder of the team and myself was bewilderment, and a feeling of being a little let down. Why would you choose to work in a part time job rather than attend your own grand final?

Some people just don't buy into the team and that's something that constantly needs to be managed. Did these members give 100%, No. Did they or will they receive 100% support from their team mates either inside the team or outside? Probably not.

It's up to you, take ownership of how much you commit to a

team and be accountable to them for that. Because if you give 100% to the team you will find that they will give 100% back to you, both within the team structure and outside it as well.

To those that don't get it and don't commit. It's no big deal, but there isn't really a place for you on a high performing team in a n ongoing sense.

Because we won the Premiership and the Championship our team will progress to the next division in the coming season. Will we be able to accept team members who are half hearted? I don't think that's going to be a good experience for anyone.

If your work team gets a big win and you progress to the next level how can you make certain you remain in the team for the next level?

Commit 100%.

What does that look like?

Give everything you can, if you have a skill gap, then fill it on the off season. If you need to be fitter for the next season, then start training early, if you need a mentor to keep up then get one.

Assess, plan and get into action.

When things don't go as planned

Have you noticed that whenever you are striving for something that's a bit beyond you, life seems to throw up all sorts of obstacles?

Whether you are pursuing the next level in your career, your relationship, your sport or whatever ceiling you are attempting to push though, every obstacle that could get in the way seems to. And it feels like you are taking 1 step forward and 2 steps back.

The good news is that this is an entirely normal occurrence for anyone wanting to grow, change or upscale.

And it's hideous.
You feel like you aren't really making progress. Or you feel like you are being taken off track, or sometimes it feels like a brick wall that you are not quite certain how to handle.

I came across a cool idea that has helped me and my clients in this situation.

Breakdown to Breakthrough

It's called Break down to breakthrough, and I've created a breakdown formula to go through whenever I'm having a bad day, or I'm feeling like I'm hitting a wall.

Here are the instructions.
First step: You are not going to fix anything right now. Your first job is to simply identify where the breakdown is. You may be thinking. I know what it is. One of my team is being a jerk. Or the boss is riding us a little too hard.

The problem with most of these initial assessments is that you are giving up any power to do anything about them. You are acting like a victim, and playing below the line. "it's someone else's fault" is the track that's playing in your head. Examine it closely, dig a bit deeper and see if you feel like you have the power to make a positive change in the script that you are running currently.

Once we've identified what this feeling is all about then we are going to prioritize and handle whatever needs handling.

There's a bit of a catch here. More often than not there wont be an urgent situation that needs handling from this. Simply identifying what going on is handling the issue.

This process turns peoples mindsets around quite quickly. For me I notice that within an hour my mood has lifted, I'm clear about what's causing it and if action needs to be taken then I'm underway. I'm taking responsibility for my mood and that puts me in the pilots seat again... I'm back above the line.

So lets use the break down formula to go a little deeper.

Initially, start writing down your ideas about what it could be under each section, just empty your thoughts onto paper. Do a data dump about what's bothering you right now. We find that sometimes the source of this feeling is in one area and white often it's in all three areas. It can be work related or personal. You are a whole human being and your brain doesn't distinguish and differentiate your emotions like we segment our days.

Then go back over your notes and start to highlight the big ones. You'll find that the more you right the more you become clear about what the real source of your breakdown is.

The source of your frustration is going to be one of these things.

Sometimes it's all three.

1. A thwarted goal

This is a goal you said you intended to have achieved but haven't and you feel something or someone is thwarting you getting there.

1.
2.
3.
4.
5.
6.
7.

2. An unmet expectation

This is all about your own expectations. What are the expectations that you have set up in your mind that are not happening. Sometimes these expectations are unsaid and unexamined. We often grow up with a set of expectations from our parents or our culture and they sit in the back of our brain measuring the world according to them.

What unmet expectations are currently swimming around in your head?

1.
2.
3.
4.
5.
6.

3. A withhold

This is something you should have said or done but haven't. A situation that you need to handle but have not.

1.
2.
3.
4.
5.

6.

Prioritize
What needs to be handled now?

1.
2.
3.

Action
What is the first action that you need to take to handle the situation or to get back above the line and take responsibility?

Chapter 11

COGNITIVE BIAS, AUTOMATIC BEHAVIOURS AND HANDLING VOLATILE AND UNCERTAIN EVENTS

The Drunk Monkey mind.

Have you ever had the experience of waking up at 4am, you are tired and want to go back to sleep but your brain has kicked into gear… You are awake…And what does your brain then do?

It descends into a chaotic mess of thoughts, worries and what I best describe as a drunk monkey mind. My thoughts drunkenly stumbling from one problem to another. Nothing is resolved, clarified or useful, then it suddenly lurches to the next drama. Like the movie Jumper with the hero unceremoniously pulled through to the next dimension not quite knowing what he'll have to contend with when he lands.

Occasionally you'll become so restless that you give in, get up and watch some rubbish television until it's morning and the drunken monkey has worn itself out.

I have not ever been able to either control this or do anything about what's happening in my mind. My only strategy has been to hope that I don't have one of those nights too often.

I've discovered that this is very, very common, especially amongst high performing individuals. And I've tried many strategies to manage it.

I've had instruction and suggestions from well-meaning medical doctors, psychologists, coaches, friends, mentors and loved ones. Nothing has made an impact... Until now.

Recently I learnt a simple but profound idea that has changed all of that.

The result is that I sleep better, wake up more energised and enjoy greater control over this most unwanted guest. And there are a few more very positive and unintended side effects that help me tap dance throughout my day.

When you are leading a team you will find these kinds of concerns creeping into your relaxation time. And if you are like most leaders these thoughts may become distracting during your work as well.
When you understand what's happening and how to handle it, you'll find yourself becoming a more effective leader.

Before I tell you about more it, I want to describe what it's not.

Louis Theroux and his weird weekends
One of my favourite guilty pleasures is to watch the documentary film maker Louis Theroux from the BBC, especially his series Weird Weekends.

Recently I was transfixed with his episode exploring why so many westerners travel to India in search of spiritual enlightenment. He met some pretty spaced out and weird people who were all in search of the same thing I was seeking at 4am in the morning. Peace...... What I recognised is that they were also seeking sanctuary from the barrage of drunk monkey thoughts that appear to plague the modern mind.

Many of the encounters he filmed were extremely uncomfortable interactions with what I can best describe as space cadets. These people were, far, far away from my world of high performing, brilliant minded people out to make a significant dent in the universe. They were giving the idea of taming the continuous commentary of their minds a bad reputation.

These whacky western dentists, accountants and yoga teachers, blissed out in a state of wonderment and awe as they immersed themselves in their spiritual enlightenment is what most people think of when they describe mindfulness. Zany characters wrapped in orange togas with a far away look on their face and who are apparently incapable of human communication at a basic level, let alone taking responsibility for serious business.

They seem to descend into indecipherable gibberish and jargon when asked about their journey, which seems further and further away from any practical and meaningful system of managing myself. Awakening consciousness and pain bodies and blah, blah, blah.

This is not going to help me tame my drunk monkey and keeping me performing my day job at a high level.

Ego & Quantum Physics
One day I was struggling with a problem in my business and my coach said to me... "That's just your ego getting in the way"
Wait... What?

My ego?

But I'm not some rampaging rock star demanding that all the blue m&m's are removed and vast bottles of Bollinger Champaign are in my dressing room. What's ego got to do with it?

He replied….Go read a book called A New Earth by Eckhart Tolle and then come back to me with what you understand ego to be.

The rock star persona in all its forms is what my mum taught me about ego. When you think you are some big shot and treat others around you like they are you servants, that's ego. When you are mouthing off to everyone who will listen how great you are, that's ego. And when you get big headed in anyway, that's ego.

So it seems my mums version of ego is describing a more petulant teenager than anything else. And it seems to have a strong element of self-promoting megalomaniac about it.

That's not who I am, and I really didn't understand how ego is contributing to the problem I needed solving in my business right now. What's ego got to do with it?

And then I read the book. And I understood why it's sold over 5 million copies and been favourably reviewed by some very high achievers, including Oprah and Jim Carey.

Before I take on the task of explaining how I began to loosen the grip of ceaseless thinking on my life I want to make a little agreement with you. It's really difficult to explain what comes next, and at least initially you are going to resist this change in thinking.

The agreement I'd like you to make with me right now is that

you resist making assumptions about what you know is true and when this resistance enters your thoughts, telling you this is all crap, just replace it the thought with, this could be interesting and useful. So are we in agreement?
Good. Read on.

When I asked a friend how he explained to people how he managed to quieten the commentary track in his head he replied, it's probably easier to describe quantum physics than it is to explain the ego. And effective methods to tame it's influence tend to appear light weight at first.

But that's what I'm about to attempt.

So here I go.

Quantum theory is the theoretical basis of modern physics that explains the nature and behaviour of matter and energy on the atomic and subatomic level. And to some extent the nature of reality and objectivity through the Copenhagen interpretation of quantum physics, where an object cannot be assumed to have specific properties, or even to exist, until it is measured. In short, objective reality does not exist.

This translates to a principle called superposition that claims that while we do not know what the state of any object is, it is actually in all possible states simultaneously, as long as we don't look to check. It is the measurement itself that causes the object to be limited to a single possibility.

O.K. That's easier to explain than what I'm about to describe. So buckle up your seatbelt.

We are Sentient Beings

Man is described as a Sentient being.
That means we are an animal aware of our surroundings and capable of feeling at least pleasure and pain. We are

capable of consciousness.

The concept of a being (as in a human being) is available when 5 elements are available

1. matter,
2. sensation,
3. perception,
4. mental formations and
5. consciousness. (the state of being aware of and responsive to ones surroundings)

So underneath all the buffed and polished exterior we are a Sentient Being.

And we have many anatomical systems to help that Being get around and exist.

The Circulatory system, Lymphatic system, respiratory system, nervous system, Digestive system just to name a few. Their job… to keep us alive and kicking.

Like many in the western education system I grew up with the philosophical notion "I think therefore I am."

This simple test devised to answer the question , How do I know I exist, effectively elevated the Mind to the king of all systems, the boss, the big cheese the one that we can't do without.

And while that's true from an anatomical perspective there is a structural part of the mind called the ego which really seems to run the show.

But in reality the mind is just a part of the nervous system. You may as well say. I digest therefor I am, or I circulate therefore I am, or best of all I breath therefore I am.

We have elevated the mind to such a level that our western society has often been described as a mind identified culture. We forget that underneath all the thinking we are a conscious sentient being.

Sometimes the minds drunk monkey approach to thinking is not very resourceful to simply living and handling your team mates.

It's only thinking that makes it so.

I'm paraphrasing Shakespeare here. But....
An event is just an event. An interaction is just an interaction. It is neither good or bad, right or wrong, advantageous or disastrous. It is only thinking that makes it so..... and guess who is doing the thinking. My ego.

For most of my life I had been at the mercy of my ego, the drunk monkey, for the interpretation of events and interactions that happened to me each day.

For example
My wife said this, that must mean.......
This girls laughed at me when they looked in this direction. What wrong with me, do I look weird?
My boss was kind of rude this morning, what have I done to upset him?
Mum is always talking about my brothers achievements, she must think I'm a failure.
Last time someone spoke to me like this I was out of a job within the week.

I was beginning to see the thoughts for what they were. Just quantum bursts of energy.

And I was beginning to look at the day to day events in a very different way.

They had no inherent meaning, no link to a past or future event. They were what they were. Just an interaction, just an phone call, comment, accident, request or an action.

The guy who overtook me on the way to work, pulled in front of me and then slowed down wasn't an asshole who was a blight to conscientious drivers everywhere. He wasn't out to make my day difficult. He just overtook me, pulled into my lane and slowed down…. Who knows why. Or what thoughts were going on in his head or why he took the action he did. I can be fairly sure of one thing though. It probably had nothing to do with me. And even more certain of another thing. If I gave this much thought, labelled it with some sort of meaning and then chose to put up some resistance.

The only person who would be negatively affected by this is ME!

Let that sink in for a moment. Thinking about this event and giving it meaning was winding up my drunk monkey, who in turn was ruining my morning drive to work.

Instead of being relaxed and enjoying my surroundings I was wound up tight, clenching my jaw, tensing the muscles in my shoulders and gripping the steering wheel in frustration. I was doing this to myself. And I was doing this my merely thinking about it. What a waste of time. What a waste of energy….What a waste of this precious day.

It was only thinking that made it so.
And the guy directing the thinking was the drunk monkey running around in my head.

Then a profound thought struck me. That's just not helping

me. And now I know exactly why.

What happened next was a clarity that I hadn't experienced before.

I was not living right here, right now. I was reacting in an unconscious way.

My mind was obsessed with the meaning that I had given to all the events like this in the past, and I was reacting to them now like a reflex. Giving them the meaning that I had decided long ago was correct for this event. Like your knee involuntarily jerking when the Doc taps on your nerve I was acting on an involuntary reflex, based on a behaviour that I had long ago decided was appropriate.

To be unconscious means to react automatically. Without taking account of the present circumstances making a conscious decision based on what was happening here, now.

I'd experienced what it was to be unconscious before. For example when on a long car journey and suddenly I notice that I've changed lanes on the freeway and taken the exit to the destination, but I don't remember consciously making the decision to do so. You might just describe it as being lost in thought.

Or when I'm playing in a band and suddenly find myself at the final verse thinking, what happened to 2nd and 3rd, did I miss them? But I was lost in thought about my gear, or the sound system or what my bandmates were wearing. All the time my mind was elsewhere. I was on autopilot.

What it boils down to is that while my body was in one place, my mind was somewhere else altogether. That's the definition of unconscious. And being unconscious can be kind of dangerous for your body.

The result of being unconscious is not only physical harm to me, but reacting unconsciously to events in my day can be just as harmful. Allowing automatic behaviours which were developed and installed into the software of my brain a long time ago to govern the current situation is at best, not helping me. And possibly actively sabotaging what I want to accomplish in a day, a career or a life.

Holy crap I've been on autopilot for a long time!
Giving meaning to circumstances they did not deserve and holding onto that meaning and installing it into my day to day operating system. No wonder the monkey is drunk!

One of the most profound ideas I found in A New Earth is this.

Your ego requires chronological time to exist. It needs the memories of the past and experiences to help it create the behaviours I'm using today and to react to situations that are presented to me. It also requires the future into order to keep you on the hop, always consuming, doing, achieving. But never satiated. Forever striving because you seem to lack something in your life.

The drunk monkey continually driving you for more, then pushing the button for an automatic response to something. Never stopping, or pausing for breath, or to smell the roses. The Author Dan Harris, who wrote 10% Happier describes it like this. "The running commentary that had dominated my field of consciousness since I could remember - Was kind of an asshole"

The assumptions and actions of my mind look like this;
The past has taught me to respond to circumstances in a particular way. Every time I even get a whiff of this trigger I'll

respond like this. That's going to save me a little time. I'll just respond to everything that looks like this with reaction 7B. Actually if it's even in the same overall category of stimulus I'll stick with 7B.

For example, Everyone is out for themselves. If someone gives me something they want something in return. They want to sell me something or take advantage of me. So I'll rebuff everyone, that way I won't be tricked into buying something I don't want, or worse agreeing to something I don't want to do.

The future is going to be better when you get there. So don't stand still, keep moving, striving, wanting, consuming, because where you are right now isn't it.

For example. You'll be a success when you land that deal, or have a $1M in the bank, or that car, or holiday. And success is going to feel so good. You'll be happy, fulfilled. At peace. Finally able to stop.

Eckhart Tolle points out that the present is all we have. Or to put it another way it is always the present. We experienced our past through a long series of present moments and we'll experience the future the same way. When we live our lives we are just experiencing life one present moment at a time. And stringing those moments together is what we call our history. So what on earth would we waste those precious moments by flipping thought them automatically or pissing them away distracted by a possible future event.

I realise I had live a vast amount of my life this way. I was an impatient child, eager to get from one experience to another. Consume the next thing and move on. Always an eye on the destination and not taking in the journey. Or to use John Lennon's words. "Life is what happens to you while you are busy making other plans"

So this is what my coach meant when he said your ego is just getting gin the way.

He wasn't warning me of a percent for megalomania, he was letting me know that the way I was reacting was being ruled by my mind, my automatic reactions and a thwarted sense of my future self. And it wasn't helping me.

At this point the whole methodology of the way my mind worked was looking kind of sketchy. Like a really dumb way to live. Bound up by automatic reactions that had little bearing on current circumstances, with an insatiable desire for what was to come next. I had never learned how to get that bloody monkey to sleep. A little peace and quiet, just for a moment.

Fully present and fully conscious in practice at 4am

The Ego is tamed by being fully present in this moment right now.

The ego needs chronological time to exist. It is the fuel that feeds it.

One of the most profound lessons that was dawning on my was this. Being fully present and fully conscious was what I was made to do. It's what the Human Being was built for. And it was the secret to quieten the incessant track that had dominated my days and nights.

To quieten the drunk monkey become aware of your surroundings and your physical place in it. And the easiest way to do this is simply to notice your breathing.

So as I lay in bed at 4am with my mind starting to buzz I set my mind to become fully conscious and fully present. And if you are about to go into a situation at work or with one of your team mates it works just was well. (I know this sounds like the opposite thing you should do when you are trying to get back to sleep, or ramp up for a confrontation, but this is what works for me) First notice your breathing, feel the air entering your body. Then notice your feet, and pay attention to how every part of your body is feeling. Physically feel other sensations like the cool air being gently pushed around the room, then my breathing again. Then I notice that I'm not thinking about anything at all. And I'm back to breathing….. And then I wake up at 7am. refreshed and vibrant.

As I was working on being totally present in time, right here in my bed right now, and fully conscious of my body and surroundings, I managed to switch off my minds accounting for chronological time. I was just in the present moment. And all the thoughts that were swirling a few minutes ago ceased.

Along with that the worry, anxiety, regret and distraction stopped also. Replaced with peaceful nothingness. And, as it turns out, a really rejuvenating sleep.

That's all fine at 4am but what about in the middle of the day when I need to be at my sharpest.

This is where it gets really interesting.

It turns out that suspending my judgement of events that happen during the day gives my brain the opportunity to find new and sometimes radically different solutions. Which is really, really valuable to my clients.

Elite sportspeople call it maintaining a Blue head. If you are in the middle of a big game hot emotions often get in the way of clear thinking and resourceful decision making. That's what's called a Red head. So these athletes will do whatever they need to do to get rid of the red head.

And in the middle of a heavy physical match this can be difficult to maintain.

In the middle of running a business, or leading a team it can also be very difficult to keep a Blue head also. Keeping your minds chatter in its rightful place is a very effective way to achieve this.

Being fully present and conscious means that when I'm working with people I'm operating at a much higher level, free from the distractions of my automatic reactions or any anxiety about the future. Again, client s like that sort of thing.

I arrive at my destination fully charged
and invigorated because I have let go of any thoughts or beliefs that could otherwise zap me of energy.

And most amazing of all, when my energy is up, my focus is clear and my mind ready to work, people are attracted to that. They must sense it, because I've seen that in other people lives too. When their outlook is distracted, desperate and needy people are repelled, But when they are
fully conscious, present and aware people must have a desire to connect. I've found that in this very positive state I attract a significantly higher quality of client, opportunities and far more interesting work.

Jeremy and the giant contract
Recently one of my clients, Jeremy, called me in quite a bit of distress. He was a brilliant software engineer who is running a highly innovative business and had just received some bad news. The project he was about to start on was put on hold because of a restructuring at the clients end. The MD who championed the project had decided to leave and had called to say, don't start until you've received the first payment, just to be safe.

An event happened in his day.

He then reacted in the same way he had so many times before when a project began to fall apart. Projecting backwards, self-recrimination about what he didn't do right, contracts not being watertight or timelines not being urgent enough. Then his mind raced forward to the future and what it would mean. That's the next 3 months income gone, now how will pay my staff, and without the security of this job that means I want be able to start on my speculative job. Around and around his mind would have gone in identifying all that this means and the ramifications. His particular drunk monkey kept him awake for about 3 nights, and with very little sleep and several ongoing jobs that needed his attention, this just wasn't helpful.

He was unconscious. His body may have been sitting in his office, but his mind was elsewhere.
That's not much help. And it's especially not very resourceful to finding solutions to manage this event.

First step, let's get the facts out.
- The job was not cancelled, there was a change of management within the company.
- This project was going to have a massive impact on the marketing of a strong business and they had not implemented any alternative
- Retail businesses that don't create marketing campaigns go out of business really quickly, so they likely needed this project sooner rather than later
- And in a time of instability this project could provide the stability the team needed to transition to new management.

No judgment, no emotions. Just the facts
Notice the reactions, thoughts and scenarios that your ego is pushing on you. They aren't necessarily true, accurate or appropriate for this situation.

If all Jeremy does right now is to observe his thoughts then he will have taken the sting out of the ego control over the situation.

We then went on to develop a plan of action to determine how soon the payment would be made and what the next possible steps were. A whole range of options opened up for Jeremy when he let go of the reactions he was hijacked by and started to respond to the event in a creative way.

To summarise what I had discovered about my ego..

1. Non judgment; Cease labelling events and giving them meaning they do not yet have. Allow events to just be events.
2. Non-resistance; Observe and then respond, rather than react based on automatic behaviours.
3. Non alignment; Align the success of your day with your ability to be fully present, conscious and doing your best to contribute positively by adding value.
4. Let it go; If it's not helping me let it go. Is this resourceful for me right now? If not leave it.
5. Assume good intent; Don't make others wrong
6. When I quieten it down and just breath (or do a breathing meditation) I am less stressed or wound up during the day.

Let go of the red head – Practical strategies to handle emotions

1. Recognise that your mind is just another system. It's not who you are so stop taking it so seriously.

2. The past and the future are just a collection of present moments strung together. Don't waste this moment right now. Experience it fully by becoming fully conscious of what you are doing.
3. There is no pre-ordained meaning to events that happen to you throughout the day. They are just events, it's only your thinking that gives them meaning, either good or bad. So look at what happens to you today without judgement or giving it undue meaning, you might just see something completely different.
4. Let it go. If most events are just occurrences without specific significance, then the only person being disadvantaged by it is you… So LET IT GO.

Why Kung Fu Panda is so cool and how to master the present.

What's happening?
This is a question that will bring you back to the present time, and drag you out of automated behaviour.

If you are freaking out about a tough meeting or confrontation you must have then try this.

Do a fact report.
Just stick to the facts… Because solutions lie in the facts.. Are you worried about the emotion and the drama? Well perhaps you could see it for what it is… Just an ego state that has no possibility for either taking responsibility or making good decision.

So if your counterpart is getting emotional, bring it back to the facts, and keep doing that. Even if you have to keep doing it over and over. If he gets emotional, just keep coming back to facts, because all solutions lie here and all emotions will lead you to is problems.

You'll need to notice your own behaviour. You may have some emotional response to what's going on... Just be the watcher of your own emotions, be curious about why you are having this response, where does that come from, what trigger in your mind sent you into that response... Isn't that interesting.

In Kung Fu Panda, one of my all-time favourite movies, the master Shifu was a worrier, always concerned that an event was either good or bad. If something didn't happen as it should have we lost his lolly. But his very wise senior master, Oogway, (he was known as the greatest kung fu master in history), looked at things a little differently. He didn't look at an event as either good or bad, he just accepted it as it was.

"Quit. Don't quit, Noodles, don't noodles. You are too concerned with what was and what will be" Oogway - Kung Fu Panda

This is acceptance of the present and is an essential part of operating at the highest levels of human capacity. Why? If you are operating from old automated behaviours then you are no better than an old out of date computer program running it's script without any connection to the fact that the environment it is working in has changed.

An old script (or automated behaviour) has nothing to do with what going on in front of you right now.

And emotions, especially in work related human communications can be like that, an anchor to a past that has no relevance to what is happening right now.

The real secret... Accept what is happening right now, Neither good or bad, positive or negative... It's just happening.

Accept it and be the watcher of your own response, thinking and emotions.

You may say to me that this is giving up control is in some way weaker. I'd suggest that being fully present (not giving in to automated behaviours from the past), aware (watching and observing your own mind at work) and in a state of non-judgment gives you more power than you can imagine. You are no longer a slave to the circumstances around you or the environment you find yourself in. You can respond to the moment based on the facts and what is required of you.

By not being too concerned with the past or what will be, you'll discover solutions, where once problems stood.

By challenging your cognitive bias and the way you automatically handle this kind of situation you will find innovative solutions.

Chapter 12

LEGACY
TAP DANCE TO WORK

I'd like to take a shot at redefining what success looks like at work.

Because it seems to be vastly different depending on who you talk to... And those who talk the loudest seem to be telling us that success in work has a specific look and feel, and I'm not sure that's entirely healthy.

The most salient and high profile people in this area seem to define success at work based on your net worth or how many Zillions of dollars you have created and made.

I want to propose a different measure of success.

One that is intrinsically more satisfying.
More easily attained and Infinitely more useful to the regular inhabitants of spaceship earth.

Put quite simply... How to tap dance to work!

I'm not much of a tap dancer, I'm better at Rocking to work. And when I'm playing my guitar, with my band, my teammates... I'm quite simply floating to work.

I grew up with the traditional notion that work was something you endured. Then you retired and enjoyed life.

To plie onto that idea, I'm Australian... so we don't just work.... We work hard. And play hard... The more the better.

Because we are a nation of brilliant mongrels, we make it our mission to do most things just a little bit harder, better, stronger, longer and more out there than nearly any other nation.

And what that means at work is we boast about doing long hours and claim a victory doing an all-nighters. That makes us tough. Worthy of respect. And more often than not if you talk to someone who is financially successful they'll tag onto the story how many hours they worked or how many years they went without holidays... The result. We tend to connect success with hard work, long hours and sacrifice of who we really are... and for what.. the vain hope that we'll be able to enjoy the fruits of our sacrifice in our advanced years...

What if there was another paradigm for success... another definition?

And if that success could be achieved now rather than after years of toiling long hours

I'd like to propose and alternative..... That success is about tap dancing to work.

I'd like to acknowledge meaning and purpose in what we do every day.

Humans have been grappling with this for a long time

A little over 1800 years ago a man wrote the following…….
At the break of day, when you are reluctant to get up, have this thought ready to mind: I am getting up for a man's work. Do I still resent it, if I am going out to do what I was born for, the purpose for which I was brought into the world? Or was I created to wrap myself in blankets and keep warm? But this is more pleasant? Were you then born for pleasure - All for feeling, not for action? Can you not see the plants, birds, ants, spiders, bees all doing their own work each helping in their own way to order the world? [5.1 Meditations]

Those words were written by Marcus Aurelius when he was the emperor of the Roman empire around the year 165 AD. He was about the same age as I am now when he wrote that.

His simplest statements of what he calls Man's proper work, or Mans purpose is that "man was made to do good" Or as one of the greatest leaders Frances Hesselbein puts it. "To serve is to live"

Nearly two millennia ago this man articulated the principal ideology that I would like to finish this book with.

What gets you out from under those blankets each day and how do we tap dance to work has a direct link to how you can fulfil your purpose on spaceship earth.

Gratitude, Goals and Grace

These are three principals that I have come to rely on as I

personally journey through my life.
- Looking in the rear view mirror and feeling gratitude for what is
- Gazing forward and developing meaningful pathways forward,
- Being present . Avoiding unconscious reactions and behaviours that are not resourceful to handling situations in front of me every day.

In summary. Learn from the past, allow the future to motivate you now and avoid automated behaviours

These questions I ask myself form the core of my own purpose.
- How can I inspire others to experience meaning, happiness and success in their work?
- How could I help others to actively achieve their purpose and work from a highly motivating place?
- How can I continue to tap dance to work so that I fulfil my purpose?
- How can I attract more good things….. keep my energy up and stay on mission

An energised life - How to Tap Dance to Work

On a recent trip to Bali I was being shown through a family compound, a place where several generations of the family lived. It was basic, the kitchen was a grass covered area, open to the elements on 2 sides, with a small gas burner for a stove. They cook once a day here for the entire family. The bathrooms were not much more than holes in the ground with screens for privacy. To invest in the families future they raised pigs, fattening them up for sale, the money from which would further enrich the family's life.

As I stood, taking in the traditions and customs of this family

I was overwhelmed by how affluently we live at home in Australia.

My children play the latest video games, have high speed internet connecting them to their friends locally and internationally. Our homes are plush with luxury and our education system prepares us for a life of even more affluence and attainment.

Holidays, connivance, toys, leisure activities, financial security and a system government that will take care of our health and wellbeing should anything go awry.

I live in a culture, only a few hours by plane, but a million miles from where I was currently standing. Affluent, educated, autonomous and pampered.....Yet so many people in my home country feel a deep sense of Lack. Like they are missing out on something, or have somehow not succeeded.

They are not rich, famous or powerful... Success, by the western definition, it seems, has alluded them.

I'd like to take a shot at redefining what success looks like at work.

Because it seems to be vastly different depending on who you talk to... And those who talk the loudest seem to be telling us that success in work has a specific look and feel, and I'm not sure that's entirely healthy.

I want to propose a paradigm shift in the definition of success. an alternative view that is infinitely easier to attain, and far more satisfying than our current model.

What science now knows is that there is far greater depth to living a satisfied life than simply acquiring more money and power.

My quest has led me to discover deep meaning, purpose and fun in what I do every day.

And led me to some very, very handy tools to maintain focus, energy and excitement every day.

It is especially important in the work I do building culture in the workplace and in teams. In my experience it is in teams that so many us get to do our best work.

These tolls are the foundations for building great culture, whether it's at work, in your family or your community.

- Purpose
- Autonomy
- Mastery
- Relationships
- Flow experiences
- A growth mindset &
- Maintaining energy, presence and focus

Did you notice that money is not on that list? What research has now shown us is that as long as our basic financial needs are taken care of and we feel we are being paid fairly for our work, then the drive to make more money is a long way down the list of motivators.

After my experience in Bali I understood that more money, toys, experiences and affluence was not the recipe for an energised life. So what was?

I started to wonder....How could I increase my energy and focus to attract more good things in life?
Greater purpose, deeper relationships, more depth to my skills and increasing levels of personal *and financial* autonomy.

What could I take responsibility for and act upon to live a life of greater depth and satisfaction?

What are the daily disciplines I could do that would deal with this sense of lack and attract opportunities to fulfil a wonderful purpose on spaceship earth?

For me there are 3 elements
- Looking in the rear view mirror - Gratitude
- looking forward to the road ahead - Goals, The magic question, activating your RAS (Reticular Activating System)
- And Acceptance of the present - Grace, Consciousness and Presence

Despite many of us living in extremely affluent cultures Anxiety and depression appear to be at an all-time high.

Our children are suffering higher levels of medically treated mental illnesses than at any other time in history. And Adults, especially men, are being treated for these with drugs in higher numbers every year.

Suicide, anger and violence across all ages and genders is on the rise and a feeling of intense dissatisfaction seems to be creeping into our media rich culture.

In my country suicide is at alarming rates, especially amongst men. Seven men a day will voluntarily end their lives, every day.

Consider that 7 men will take their lives today, and another 7 tomorrow, and every day this week. And every week this year. Until Australia will have lost 2500 men this year.
I'm desperately sad to say, those figures are rising every year.

If we believe that in a great team we don't ever let our mates down, then unfortunately we are not doing well enough.

I cannot understand what it must be like to be in a place where death looks like the best alternative. It must be isolating beyond anything I can imagine. It must be hell.

Meaningful work has been shown to be core to the identity of both men and women, but especially men. And I can't help but wonder if our workplace culture is letting our team mates down. If we are ignoring developing a supportive culture where everyone gets to do fulfilling work that brings joy and meaning to their lives, are we letting our mates down?

How can you help?
Pass this book onto someone, talk to them about some of the aspects of building great teams that inspire you... And then get into action.

Do something about it.

ABOUT THE AUTHOR

Brett Odgers runs a company called Business Growth Advisors in his home town of Sydney, Australia. He has spent many years running creative businesses including photographic studios, film production companies, graphic design studios and even an advertising agency.

Brett is passionate about helping people achieve mastery in their lives and especially their business, because it creates abundance around him and makes the world a place that is a delight to live in. He continues his commitment to coaching at his local soccer club, having guided many teams to fun and success. He is currently volunteering as the director of coaching at his local club and is sharing this knowledge with many, many other teams.

Brett's business runs 12 month programs to help organisations develop and maintain high performance team culture. That program is called "Culture Eats Strategy For Breakfast" He is available for keynote speeches and workshops both in Australia and internationally. If you would like to talk to our team about how you can develop and maintain a great culture in your team contact him at business@brettodgers.com.au
To find out more go to www.businessGrowthAdvisors.com.au or www.CultureEatsStrategyForBreakfast.com.au

www.ingramcontent.com/pod-product-compliance
Ingram Content Group UK Ltd.
Pitfield, Milton Keynes, MK11 3LW, UK
UKHW021327180426
11947UKWH00017B/1482